The Doctor Cooks Soups

By Helen Chilton Kiefer, M.D., Ph.D.

*Sinfully delicious food, in large
satisfying portions,
that happens to be good for you*

The Doctor Cooks
Childstone Publishers and Productions
Oak Park, Illinois

Acknowledgments

This book is dedicated to Steven, Lesa and Scott Kiefer. Additional thanks to Steve for all the long hours of calculating and formatting recipes. Thanks for my Olney, Illinois friends for taste testing. especially Cher Hendricks, and to nurses at many hospitals who suggested recipes with their excellent cooking.

For correspondence:

The Doctor Cooks
130 N. Cuyler Ave.
Oak Park, IL 60302

©Helen C. Kiefer, M.D., Ph.D., 2000
Book cover and back design by Steven Kiefer
Cover photography by Carolyn Wright
The Photography Studio, Santa Fe, NM

ISBN 0-9706384-0-X

Soups The Forgotten Treasure

"Sinfully delicious food, in large satisfying portions, that happens to be good for you." That's the motto of this cookbook. Now you can **eat** to grow healthy, not deprive yourself. How about a soup that tastes like a large Pizza Supreme, complete with gooey cheese? Or the unusual, but delicious Bacon Lettuce and Tomato soup of southern plantation fame? Or the innovative Cheeseburger Soup? No need to order potatoes on the side--they're already in it! All these and more are at your fingertips inside **The Doctor Cooks Soups**.

But that's just the beginning. Let's not forget the Italian influence on soup, as in Italian Beef Soup with Two Peppers, Lasagna Soup, or the elegant Osso Bucco (veal shank) Soup. Or how about the Oriental influence on soups, as in Salmon Teriyaki Soup, Green Chili Egg Drop Soup, in which east meets west, the elegant Plum Chicken Soup, Hot and Sour Fresh Tuna Soup and Tom Yung Thai Shrimp Soup. Or the Latin influence found in Brazilian Black Bean Soup with Bananas, Southwest Turkey Stew, Taco Soup and Cuban Chicken Rice Soup. Elegant meal-size soups are included as well, like Broccoli Chicken Divan, various Mediterranean seafood stews, and Beef Burgundy Soup. Hearty meal sized soups include Georgia Brunswick Stew, Czechoslovakian Pork Goulash Soup, and Tuna Casserole Soup.

Please feel free to browse the table of contents in the next several pages to see a description of these and other delicious soups, a total of 75 in all. Soups to warm you in winter, sometimes to cool your summer, and always to taste great, satisfy your appetite, and guard your health.

The Doctor Cooks soups contain a significant number of vegetables, and often even fruits, in a very palatable fashion, with all the healthy vitamins, fiber, and many of the newly discovered "phytochemicals," which are highly protective against both cancer and heart disease. For example, substances in broccoli, cauliflower and cabbage are highly protective against breast and some intestinal cancers. Tomatoes, eaten several times a week in any form, may be up to 75% effective in preventing prostate cancer, now the number one killer in men. The French have had their hearts protected against the fatty excesses in their diet by substances in red wine for thousands of years. Science is just on the threshold of discovering all the plant substances in fruits and vegetables and herbs, which protect against heart disease and cancer, our two major killers. For this reason as many protective servings of fruit and vegetables possible are built deliciously into each and every soup.

The only danger with soups, in general, is that they can be high in sodium. Some commercial soups contain a whole day's sodium allowance in one serving! Soups in **The Doctor Cooks**, however, were carefully altered to replace sodium with a multitude of flavors from nutritionally healthy sources, so you won't even miss the salt. The soups in this book are designed to be low in fat, especially saturated fats and cholesterol. They also have little in the way of refined sugars, making them ideal for those who already suffer from the heart risks of diabetes, coronary artery disease and high blood pressure. With **The Doctor Cooks** there is no trade off, you really can have it all, gourmet great taste, with satisfying portions and good health too.

There are some very good reasons to include soups with your meals. Rarely do Europeans or Asians start a meal without soup. Soup supplies graciousness to the meal, and is invariably low in calories and fat. Soup gives needed fluids in a healthful way, and, if eaten leisurely, with conversation and perhaps bread and wine, soup fills one up significantly, preventing over-eating during the more nutritionally hazardous main dish and dessert courses.

There are some even better reasons to make soup your meal! For example, a filling soup will usually have between 200 to 300 calories and negligible fat, while a main dish that might not even satisfy will have 800 to 1000 calories, or even more, and significant levels of both saturated fat and cholesterol. Soups in this book that are large enough to serve as a full, light meal are marked with an asterisk (*) by their title.

In the modern American diet, we are often told that "everything that tastes good is bad for you." It is so refreshing to find something that you can eat and enjoy while growing more healthy. And, as you get your wooden spoons and soup ladles ready, we, at **The Doctor Cooks** raise our glasses, and in the words of the ancient mealtime toast, wish you, "to life," in all it's meanings.

Soups

Avgolemono Seafood Soup- Classic Greek treatment in a lemony thick soup containing seafood and rice.

Asparagus Shrimp Soup- A gentle, gingered Chinese treatment of asparagus and shrimp.

Bacon Lettuce and Tomato Soup- A lighter variation of the original served at a plantation outside New Orleans, with all the flavors its name suggests.

Beef Burgundy Soup- A beefy whole meal stew with all the richness of slow simmering in red wine.

Bouillabaisse- Classic Mediterranean sea foods in a light tomato-white wine broth.

Brazilian Black Bean Soup With Bananas- A Brazilian favorite with chili spiced black beans and a lovely fresh banana garnish.

Broccoli Cheese Soup- Everyone's favorite, ready in 15 minutes.

Broccoli Chicken Divan Soup- A rich, creamy, lemony fresh broccoli lover's favorite with chunks of tender chicken breast.

Carrot Cheese Soup- A cheddary, creamy, carrot soup.

Carrot Tomato Squash Soup- A smooth blend of carrot and sweet squash flavors, accented with the tomato-lime-pepper tastes of American Indian Cuisine from the southwest.

Celery Lovers Soup- An intensely celery tasting creamy potato soup.

Cheeseburger Soup- A rich, cheesy, hamburger and potato soup.

Cher's California Champagne Shrimp Soup- A champagne-grapefruit citrus treatment of shrimp with julienne fresh green beans.

Chicken-Lentil Mulligatawny Soup- A favorite British Colonial Indian Soup, mixing the rich tastes of lentils, dark chicken meat, curry and mint.

Chicken-wild rice Soup- A creamy rich thick soup of chicken, mushrooms and wild rice.

Chicken with 40 cloves of Garlic Soup- A so good for you and delicious French classic soup.

Chinese Egg-Drop Peapod Soup- A light classic Chinese soup with surprising crispness added by water chestnuts and peapods.

Chinese Hot and Sour Fresh Tuna Soup- A variation of a classic hot and sour soup from North Chinese cuisine, made with fresh tuna slivers.

Country Captain Chicken Soup- A British tomato chicken curry from colonial India.

Crab Gumbo Soup- Louisiana richness in slow cooked vegetables, rich gumbo sauce, and crab.

Cranberry Fruit Soup- A red wine-enhanced version of a chilled cranberry soup.

Creamy Vegetable Chowder- Mushrooms, squash, and red bell peppers in a buttery creamy chowder.

Cuban Chicken Rice Soup- A Cuban blend of chicken breasts, black olives, and a rich tomato taste.

Cucumber Dill Soup- An excellent chilled summer soup--cucumbers with hints of buttermilk and sour cream.

Curried Chicken Cheese Soup- A blend of chicken in a sweetly spiced creamy cheddar base.

Czechoslovakian Pork Goulash Soup- Chunks of pork, sauerkraut and sour cream with traditional paprika-caraway seed spicing.

Easy Shrimp Bisque- A smooth mellow sherry-flavored cream of shrimp soup.

Flemish Beef Stew- Beef in a traditional very rich gravy made from caramelized onions and beer.

French Peasant Soup- A robust, full soup that makes a complete and filling meal by adding "a loaf of bread and a jug of wine." Ready in 15 minutes, and freezes well.

Fresh Tomato Soup- A smooth room temperature soup with all the goodness of fresh tomatoes, and a tangy goat cheese-crouton garnish.

Fruit Soup- A light rosy chilled sweet soup with fresh fruits.

Georgia Brunswick Stew- A southern favorite of tender-cooked shredded chicken and pork, fragrant in a catsup-lemon based stew.

German Omelet Consommé- An elegant clear soup with little square ham omelets in it.

Green Chili - Egg Drop Soup- East meets west in this favorite-- you can vary it from no heat at all to fiery hot.

Honeydew Melon Soup- A chilled summer soup flavored with kiwi and honey.

Indian Tomato Rasam Soup- Yellow split peas, tomatoes and fresh coriander blend in this elegant vegetarian soup.

Italian White Bean Soup (Pasta Fazool)- The classic rich Italian white bean soup with vegetables and pasta.

Italian Beef Soup With Two Peppers- Pepperoncini and softly stewed green pepper flavor the traditional shredded Italian beef.

Italian Fish Soup (Cioppino)- The classic Mediterranean seafood stew, a whole meal in a soup bowl.

Italian Minestrone- A tomato broth with all the classic Italian vegetables.

Italian Osso Bucco (Veal Shank) Soup- A rich and garlicky rendition of a classic Italian veal dish.

Japanese Buckwheat Noodle Soup- Lightly gingered broth with the traditional buckwheat noodles served over finely sliced crisp, raw vegetables.

Jellied Madrilène Gazpacho Soup- Crunchy garden vegetables, chunks of tomatoes, all mixed with a jellied madrilène base. An excellent cold soup for summer.

Lasagna Soup- A clever blend of mushroom marinara sauce, spinach ricotta "filling" and lasagna noodles in a soup.

Margarita Shrimp Soup- A tequila and lime treatment of shrimp soup.

Mexican Shrimp Soup- Crispy with tortilla strip--A soup from the coast of Mexico with plenty of shrimp and crispy tortilla strips.

New Orleans Shrimp Soup- An unusual creamy shrimp chowder with fresh spinach and liqueur flavoring.

Orange Orange Roughy Chowder- A very unusual non-fishy fish stew with Cajun spicing, orange juice and pecans.

Oysters Rockefeller Soup- An oyster chowder-like soup, creamy, rich, with all the ingredients and flavors of oysters Rockefeller.

Pad Thai Soup- A pork shred-clear rice noodle soup, reminiscent of its namesake, with bean sprouts, omelet strips and peanut garnish.

Pizza Supreme Soup- Pepperoni, mushrooms, mozzarella, black olives, green peppers and noodles in a tomato-pizza sauce.

Plum Chicken Soup- A delicious blend of tender chunks of chicken breast and fresh plums, all in a sweet and sour sauce of balsamic vinegar and brown sugar.

Portuguese Steamed Mussel Soup- A lemon-white wine based mussel stew.

Raspberry Chicken Soup- An unusual creamy chicken fresh raspberry soup.

Renee's Herbed Vegetable Cheese Soup- Best of a number of recipes for everybody's favorite, a creamy cheese vegetable soup.

Roasted Carrot Ginger Soup- A fresh tasting roasted carrot soup with hints of oriental spices and crisp ginger topping.

Roasted Pepper Soup with Goat Cheese- A fiery blend of peppers and green tomatoes, garnished with goat cheese.

Roasted Red Pepper Soup (Garnished With Cilantro Pesto)- A beautiful rosy colored soup with a green and white center swirl garnish.

Salmon Teriyaki Soup- A traditional teriyaki sautéed fresh salmon soup with tiny whole onions and teriyaki carrots

Santa Fe Corn Chowder- A delicious soup made with fresh corn, flavored with nutmeg and green chilies.

Sausage and Lima Soup- A hearty, satisfying baby lima bean and sausage soup.

Scallop Fettucine Alfredo Soup- A soup like its namesake, rich with cheese and garlic, studded with fresh scallops.

Southwest Turkey Stew- A cumin-mustards flavored stew of chili peppers, pinto beans, corn and chunks of turkey.

Spicy Chinese Beef Soup- A soup version of the delicious Chinese classic, Star Anise Beef.

Surprise Vichyssoise- The classic cold French potato soup with surprises of sour cream, fresh pears, and watercress.

Sweet and Spicy Spaghetti Squash Soup- A very pretty soup with bits of orange and orange-colored squash, garnished with toasted nuts.

Taco Soup- Beef, tomatoes and tortillas topped with sour cream.

Tetrazzini Turkey Soup- A cream turkey linguine soup, fragrant with marjoram and pimientos.

Texas Hash Soup- A chili powder-green pepper casserole-like soup of ground beef in a tomato rice base.

Three Bean Chili Mac Soup- A hearty tomato based chili, chock full of beans and shell macaroni.

Tofu Crab Soup- A delicious oriental blend of healthy ingredients with fresh spinach.

Tomato-Sweet Corn Chowder- A whole ear of corn grated into each creamy serving.

Tom Yung Kung Thai Shrimp Soup- A superb Thai broth with piquant lemony-hot pepper flavors, filled with shrimp.

Tortilla Soup- A south-of-the-border soup chock full of chicken, tomato, garlic and toasted tortillas, all flavored with tequila and fresh lime.

Tuna Noodle Casserole Soup- All the tastes of the favorite--tuna casserole--pimientos, noodles, mushrooms all made into a creamy soup.

Nutrition At a Glance

All the recipes in this book use our patented* "logo" labeling system which allows you to scan your eyes over a line of eight simple symbols, and instantly understand all the nutritional information otherwise presented in complex tables of numbers on the labels of foods currently sold. The ease of this system relieves the frustration of trying to understand nutritional information.

In this system, readily recognized symbols are used to represent the basic nutritional building blocks of food such as fat, carbohydrate, protein, fiber, etc. The total height of any symbol represents the entire day's allowance for that substance; **the height to which the symbol is shaded** represents the fraction of that particular substance in a single serving of a given dish. For example, if the entire symbol were shaded, it would represent an entire day's allowance of that substance in that particular serving. The following illustration would be used to depict cholesterol (symbolized by a heart) in a given serving relative to the maximum daily USDA allowance of 300 mg:

CHOLESTEROL
75 mg. = 25%

CHOLESTEROL
150 mg. = 50%

CHOLESTEROL
225 mg. = 75%

CHOLESTEROL
300 mg. = 100%

When the full array of logos is presented, substances (on the left side) such as sodium, cholesterol, fat and refined sugars are considered not so good for you. If you are on a special diet in which you are supposed to avoid certain things, for example salt, in cases of high blood pressure, you can pick out recipes at a glance that have low levels in the salt shaker. When a symbol is divided in two, the left side represents things that are generally bad for you, and the right side represents healthier and more acceptable versions of the same nutrient. Hence, the complete logo display for all required nutritional disclosure information could look as follows:

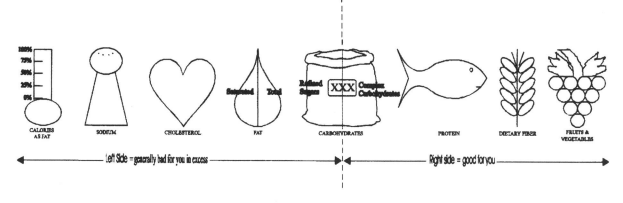

Since left is generally bad for you and right is generally good for you, you don't even need to worry about the shading of any given symbol: **a rising pattern, that is, one generally lower on**

the left and higher on the right, is sufficient information to indicate a healthier food! For example, a healthy recipe from this book might look like:

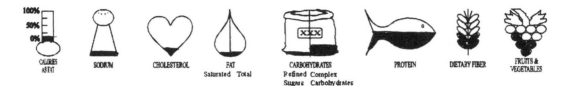

And a less healthy one for just one small burger and small fries from a fast food drive-thru restaurant might look like:

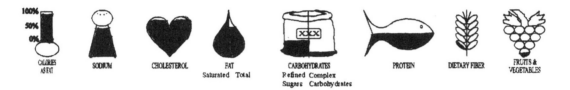

While most of the symbols are self explanatory. The two symbols on the right side bear some special mentioning. They represent "fiber" and "servings of fruits and vegetables". Thirty grams of healthful dietary fiber per day is the recommended amount. The number of fiber "seeds" shaded represent the percentage of this requirement, up to ten seeds, 100%. Latest health recommendations suggest 5 to 9 servings of fresh or cooked vegetables or fruits a day (of which only one should be potato). The number of symbolic grapes shaded represents the number of servings of fruits or vegetable (a serving is usually 1/3 to 1/2 cup) in a given serving of the food. Fruits and vegetables are increasingly viewed as important because they contain a group of substances called phytochemicals which are very protective against cancer and heart disease.

*The patent is written so as to exclude anyone else from ever using a symbol or shaded symbol to represent any nutritional quantity without paying royalties or licensing fees to The Doctor Cooks, Inc.

Avgolemono Seafood Soup

6 servings

Ingredients list

1/2	pound	of your favorite whitefish fillets * see note
6		green onions
2		cloves garlic
2	stalks	celery with leaves
1/2	cup	raw brown rice
1/2	cup	lemon juice
2		egg substitute equivalent to 2 eggs
3/4	teaspoon	salt
5	cups	water
8	ounces	clam juice (1 bottle)
1	tablespoon	olive oil
1	tablespoon	flour

*firm catfish, cod, roughy, haddock, sole, etc.

Directions

- Chop celery medium fine, mince garlic, chop green onions, white parts and green parts separately

- Heat oil in large Dutch oven over medium heat. Stir in minced garlic, celery, white parts of onions. Cook, stirring until vegetables start turning translucent and just start to brown

- Add the clam juice, water, rice and salt. Cover

- Simmer, covered over medium low heat, about 1 hour, until rice is tender and splitting open

- Cut fish into 1/2 inch chunks. Add all at once to the simmering soup. Cook, stirring occasionally, 4 to 5 minutes, until the fish is just cooked. Remove from heat

- Stir lemon juice and flour together until smooth. Stir in egg substitute

- Return soup to low heat, stir vigorously while adding the egg mixture. Cook, stirring, several minutes, until starting to thicken. Ladle into a heated bowl. Garnish with reserved chopped green onions

- Makes about 9 cups of soup, six servings of 1 1/2 cups each. 180 calories per serving

CALORIES AS FAT   SODIUM   CHOLESTEROL   FAT Saturated Total   CARBOHYDRATES Refined Complex Sugars Carbohydrates   PROTEIN   DIETARY FIBER   FRUITS & VEGETABLES

Asparagus Shrimp Soup

6 servings

Ingredients list

6	cups	chicken broth low sodium
6		Chinese or Japanese dried mushrooms * see note
2	10 oz boxes	frozen asparagus spears **see note
1	teaspoon	fresh ginger, grated
3/4	pound	fresh shrimp ***see note
1		clove garlic minced
1/4	teaspoon	red pepper flakes
1	tablespoon	vegetable oil

*soak mushrooms in hot water about 20 minutes (until softened) and cut into 1/8 inch strips
**or equal quantity fresh asparagus pieces
***peeled and raw butterflied medium shrimp with tails on

Directions

- Cut asparagus into 1 inch pieces, and pat the raw shrimp dry on paper towels

- Heat oil in medium skillet until hot. Stir in garlic, ginger, red pepper flakes and butterflied shrimp. Stir fry until shrimp just starting to turn pink. Remove from heat immediately

- Heat chicken broth in soup kettle or Dutch oven to a simmer, add mushrooms. Add asparagus and simmer 3 to 4 minutes. Stir in shrimp. garlic mixture, using rubber spatula to scrape out all ingredients

- Simmer 3 to 4 more minutes then ladle into soup bowls and serve immediately

- Makes about 9 cups, 1 1/2 cups per serving. 120 calories per serving

CALORIES AS FAT   SODIUM   CHOLESTEROL   FAT Saturated Total   CARBOHYDRATES Refined Complex Sugars Carbohydrates   PROTEIN   DIETARY FIBER   FRUITS & VEGETABLES

Bacon Lettuce and Tomato Soup

6 servings

Ingredients list

6	cups	low sodium chicken broth (or vegetable broth)
1	tablespoon	Tabasco® sauce
1	teaspoon	thyme
1	tablespoon	Worcestershire sauce
3	slices	Canadian Bacon
1	small head	iceberg lettuce
3	large	tomatoes, each cut in 12 wedges
2	slices	bread, toasted until firm
1/2	tablespoon	nonfat mayonnaise
1	tablespoon	margarine
1	tablespoon	nonfat sour cream

Directions

- Melt 1 tablespoon margarine in 8" heavy skillet

- Cut each piece of Canadian Bacon into 1/2" wide by 2" strips and fry in skillet until lightly browned

- Divide between 6 shallow, plate-sized soup bowls

- Add tomatoes into skillet and lightly fry the tomato wedges, dividing them between the six soup bowls

- After washing and patting dry, slice whole head of lettuce crossways into 3/4" thick round center slices, making 4 even round slices. Keeping the round shape, cut each into quarters and arrange the 4 quarters of each slice in the bottom of each bowl

- Place prepared bowls in warming oven

- In a saucepan heat the broth to boiling and stir in Tabasco® sauce, thyme and Worcestershire sauces. Reduce to simmer and simmer 5 minutes

- Prepare crouton garnish--spread one side of dry toast to the edges with the mayonnaise mixed with the sour cream. Cut in thirds

- Divide the simmering liquid evenly into the 6 prepared bowls, float a toast crouton on each one and serve

- Makes 6 cups per serving, 1 cups of broth plus vegetables per serving, 65 calories per serving

CALORIES AS FAT   SODIUM   CHOLESTEROL   FAT Saturated Total   CARBOHYDRATES Refined Complex Sugars Carbohydrates   PROTEIN   DIETARY FIBER   FRUITS & VEGETABLES

Beef Burgundy Soup*

6 servings

Ingredients list

1	pound	boneless chuck roast lean and trimmed
2	tablespoons	olive oil
3	cups	red wine (Merlot or Chianti)
2	medium	yellow onions
2	bunches	green onions
1	teaspoon	sugar
2		cloves garlic
2	teaspoons	thyme
2		bay leaves
2	tablespoons	flour
1/2	teaspoon	salt
1	teaspoon	fresh ground pepper
4	cups	water
1/2	pound	sliced mushrooms
4	medium	carrots
3	medium	red potatoes
2	medium	Italian plum tomatoes
1	package	(10 ounces) frozen baby peas

Directions

- Peel yellow onions, and cut into very thin wedges, separating layers. Wash and trim green onions. Chop whites and greens separately. Peel carrots and cut into chunks. Wash red potatoes and cut into chunks, leaving peel intact. Mince garlic. Coarsely chop tomatoes, removing seeds

- Cut meat into 1/2 inch by 1/2 inch by 1 inch strips. Put flour, salt, and pepper in a sealable plastic bag and shake meat in bag, gently, until all flour mixture is used. Set aside.

- Put 1 tablespoon olive oil in a Dutch oven and cook sections of yellow onions, and white parts of green onions, along with garlic over medium heat, stirring constantly until quite browned and very soft. Add sugar and cook one minute more, stirring, until nicely browned. Remove to bowl and reserve. Do not clean pan

- In same pan, add remaining tablespoon oil and brown meat over medium heat, stirring occasionally (steps 2 and 3 take some time but are essential to the flavor of the final dish). Stir in mushrooms and cook 2 to 3 minutes. Stir in onion mixture

- Remove from heat and add carrots, potatoes, tomatoes, spices, water and wine to pan. Bring to a simmer

- Cover soup tightly and simmer, stirring occasionally, over low heat until carrots and meat are fork tender, about one hour (add a small amount water if too much liquid is boiling off)

- Set the box of peas out to thaw

- Divide thawed peas evenly into heated bowls and ladle on hot soup, dividing meat, carrots, and potatoes evenly between bowls

- Sprinkle liberally with reserved chopped green onion

- Makes about 9 to 10 cups, 1 1/2 to 1 2/3 cups per serving. 435 calories per serving

| CALORIES AS FAT | SODIUM | CHOLESTEROL | FAT Saturated Total | CARBOHYDRATES Refined Complex Sugars Carbohydrates | PROTEIN | DIETARY FIBER | FRUITS & VEGETABLES |

(Beef Burgundy Soup)

Bouillabaisse*

6 servings

Ingredients list

2	pounds	firm whitefish (seabass, cod, other)
2		lobster tails *see note
1	pound	sea scallops
1	dozen	clams, well scrubbed
1	dozen	mussels, well scrubbed
16	ounces	clam juice, 2 bottles
1	bunch	green onions
6	large	Italian plum tomatoes
2		leeks, white part only
4		cloves garlic
1	teaspoon	thyme
1	teaspoon	fresh ground pepper
1	bunch	cilantro, loosely packed
2	tablespoons	olive oil
2	cups	dry white wine
4	cups	water
6	thick	French bread slices

*frozen--have butcher cut with a saw into 1/2 inch to 3/4 inch slices across the tails, making 7 to 9 "rounds" per tail

Directions

- Scrub mussels and clams. Thaw the prepared lobster tail rounds. Cut fish and scallops into 1 inch by 1 1/2 inch chunks. Refrigerate

- Chop green onions. Slice leeks thinly crosswise. Mince garlic. Wash and coarsely chop the tomatoes, removing any obvious seeds

- Put 1 tablespoon of the olive oil in a large Dutch oven over medium heat. Stir in chopped garlic, green onions and leeks. Cook, stirring, until the onions and the leeks turn translucent

- Stir in tomatoes and cilantro and cook 3 or 4 more minutes. Stir in the thyme and the pepper

- Add white wine, clam juice and water. Bring to a boil

- Add fish, lobster, scallops, clams and mussels. Cook, covered over medium low heat for 15 to 20 minute, until fish is firm and white and the mussels and clams have opened. (Discard any that are not opening in the heat)
- Meanwhile, heat the oven to 350 degrees. Use the remaining tablespoon of olive oil to brush the top and sides of 6 slices of French bread. Place on a sheet of aluminum foil on a cookie sheet and toast until just brown, 7 to 10 minutes, checking often
- Put 1 slices of toasted French bread in each of 6 heated large shallow soup bowls. Divide types of seafood evenly between the bowls. Ladle on the broth and vegetables from the pot
- Makes about 12 cups of soup, 2 cups per serving. 635 calories per serving

CALORIES AS FAT   SODIUM   CHOLESTEROL   FAT Saturated Total   CARBOHYDRATES Refined Complex Sugars Carbohydrates   PROTEIN   DIETARY FIBER   FRUITS & VEGETABLES

Brazilian Black Bean Soup With Bananas

6 servings

Ingredients list

16	ounces	black beans, canned (with liquid)
14	ounces	canned Mexican tomatoes, undrained
2	medium	yellow onions, chopped fine
3	medium	carrots
4	cloves	garlic, chopped fine
1	tablespoon	chili powder
1	teaspoon	thyme
1	teaspoon	basil
1/4	cup	dry sherry
3		ripe bananas
1	tablespoon	margarine
4	cups	water
1		lime

Directions

- Chop onions, garlic, and carrots

- Melt margarine in Dutch oven over medium heat, add onions, garlic, and carrots and cook, over low heat, stirring occasionally, about 15 minutes

- Stir in all other ingredients except bananas, lime, and sherry

- Simmer, covered, over low heat, stirring occasionally, for 1 hour. Remove from heat, stir in sherry, and cool slightly. Pour all but about 1 cup into food processor or blender, and blend lightly until coarse and grainy. Mash the remaining 1 cup soup until lumpy and combine with blended soup in Dutch oven. Heat until simmering

- Slice bananas and squeeze juice of lime over them to prevent darkening

- Ladle soup into 6 heated bowls- a serving is approximately one cup

- Float banana slices on top, and serve

- Makes about 6 cups of soup, 1 cup per serving. 360 calories per serving

CALORIES & FAT   SODIUM   CHOLESTEROL   FAT Saturated Total   CARBOHYDRATES Refined Complex Sugars Carbohydrates   PROTEIN   DIETARY FIBER   FRUITS & VEGETABLES

Broccoli Cheese Soup

6 servings

Ingredients list

1	pound	broccoli (frozen, stems and flowers, chopped)
3	cups	water
1	can	(10 1/2 ounces) Campbell's cheese soup
1/2	teaspoon	nutmeg
1	can	(12 1/2 ounces) evaporated skim milk
1/2	cup	nonfat sour cream
1	teaspoon	lemon juice
1/4	cup	cheddar cheese, lowfat

Directions

- Put 3 cups water in medium saucepan, cover and bring to a boil
- Thaw out frozen chopped broccoli slightly, then add to boiling water, along with lemon juice. Cover and simmer 8 to 10 minutes until just tender
- Stir in soup, evaporated skim milk, and nutmeg and bring to a simmer
- Remove from heat and stir in sour cream and serve sprinkled with grated reduced fat cheddar
- Makes 7 1/2 cups of soup, 1 1/4 cups soup per serving. 165 calories per serving

CALORIES
AS FAT

SODIUM

CHOLESTEROL

FAT
Saturated Total

CARBOHYDRATES
Refined Complex
Sugars Carbohydrates

PROTEIN

DIETARY FIBER

FRUITS &
VEGETABLES

The Doctor Cooks

Soups

Broccoli-Chicken Divan Soup*

6 servings

Ingredients list

2	pounds	fresh broccoli
2		skinless, boneless, chicken breast
10	ounces	Campbell's Healthy Request cream of chicken soup
1/2	cup	nonfat mayonnaise
1	can	(12 ounces) evaporated skim milk
3	teaspoons	lemon juice
1	teaspoon	curry powder
1/2	cup	lowfat cheddar cheese, coarsely grated
3	cups	water
1/4	cup	sliced almonds, lightly toasted

Directions

- Separate broccoli into large stalks with flowers attached

- Wash, but don't drain out. Arrange in microwave safe dish with water that clings to it

- Sprinkle with 2 teaspoons lemon juice and cover with microwave safe wrap

- place chicken breasts in 3 cups water in covered Dutch oven and cook over medium low heat 10 to 15 minutes, until cooked through

- During this same cooking time place prepared dish of broccoli in a microwave and steam 6 to 8 minutes, until firm but just piercable with a fork

- Remove chicken, and to broth in pan add chicken soup, mayonnaise, evaporated skim milk, curry powder, 1 teaspoon lemon juice and cheese

- Bring to a simmer over medium low heat, stirring constantly until simmering

- Slice reserved cooked chicken breasts crosswise into 1/3 inch slices and stir into simmering soup

- Remove from heat and divide evenly into heated bowls

- Arrange 2 large broccoli stalks over soup in each bowl and sprinkle with toasted sliced almonds (serve with knife and fork as well as spoon)

- Makes about 10 cups of soup, 1 2/3 cups per serving 270 calories

CALORIES AS FAT   SODIUM   CHOLESTEROL   FAT Saturated Total   CARBOHYDRATES Refined Complex Sugars Carbohydrates   PROTEIN   DIETARY FIBER   FRUITS & VEGETABLES

Carrot Cheese Soup

6 servings

Ingredients list

2	cans	carrots, w/liquid (two 14 1/2 ounce cans)
4	stalks	celery, with leafy tops
1	bunch	green onions
10 3/4	ounces	(1 can) cheddar cheese soup
1	can	(12 1/2 ounces) evaporated skim milk
2	teaspoons	thyme
1	teaspoon	ground marjoram
1/4	teaspoon	cayenne pepper
2	tablespoons	diet margarine
1/2	cup	grated lowfat cheddar or Colby cheese

Directions

- Wash then trim and chop celery (including leaves) and chop green onions

- Put diet margarine in a large nonstick Dutch oven over medium heat. Add celery and green onions and cook, stirring occasionally for 4 to 5 minutes

- Stir in carrots with their liquid, the spices, evaporated skim milk and cheese soup. Bring to a simmer, stirring occasionally

- Serve in heated bowls, sprinkled with 1 1/3 tablespoon grated cheese per serving

- Makes 7 to 8 cups soup, about 1 1/4 cups per serving. 180 calories per serving

| CALORIES AS FAT | SODIUM | CHOLESTEROL | FAT Saturated Total | CARBOHYDRATES Refined Complex Sugars Carbohydrates | PROTEIN | DIETARY FIBER | FRUITS & VEGETABLES |

Carrot Tomato Squash Soup

6 servings

Ingredients list

1	pound	carrots (about 4 large carrots)
1	pound	acorn squash
4		green onions
2	teaspoon	reduced sodium chicken or bouillon granules
6	small	Italian plum tomatoes
1/4	cup	brown sugar
1	teaspoon	curry powder
1	teaspoon	cinnamon
6	cups	water
1/4	teaspoon	red pepper flakes
1/3	cup	lowfat sour cream
1	tablespoon	diet margarine
1		lime

Directions

- Scrub, then chop carrots into chunks. Wash outside of acorn squash and quarter it, remove seeds, but leave peel on

- Put 4 cups of water in soup kettle with top. Add carrots and squash and cook, covered, over medium low heat until squash and carrots are tender and easily pierced with a fork (about 1/2 hour)

- Drain cooking liquid from vegetables. Combine with the bouillon granules and 2 additional cups of water in the soup kettle, along with carrots and peeled squash chunks.

- Chop whites and greens of onions separately. Reserve greens

- Chop tomatoes into coarse chunks and remove seeds.

- In small frying pan cook whites of onions in margarine, stirring frequently, until translucent. Add 2/3 of the tomatoes and cook another 3 to 4 minutes. Add contents of this frying pan to squash-carrot mixture and cool until warm

- Process portions of the squash-carrot-onion mixture in a blender or food processor until smooth, return to soup kettle

- Turn heat to low medium and bring soup to a simmer. Stir in brown sugar, curry powder, pepper flakes, and reserved tomatoes and chopped green onions, along with 1/4 teaspoon grated zest from the lime.

- Simmer 10 minutes, stirring occasionally, until tomatoes just softening. Squeeze the juice from the lime and stir in. Serve hot, topped with 1 tablespoon nonfat sour cream and small sliver of lime rind, if desired

- Makes about 10 cups of soup, 1 2/3 cups per serving. 180 calories per serving. It freezes and reheats well

CALORIES AS FAT   SODIUM   CHOLESTEROL   FAT Saturated Total   CARBOHYDRATES Refined Complex Sugars Carbohydrates   PROTEIN   DIETARY FIBER   FRUITS & VEGETABLES

(Carrot Tomato Squash Soup)

Celery Lovers Soup
6 servings

Ingredients list

4	stalks	celery with leaves
1	bunch	green onions
2	large	carrots
1	package	(8 ounces) hashed brown potatoes
1	can	(10 1/2 ounces) cream of celery soup
1	can	(12 ounces) evaporated skim milk
1/2	cup	grated reduced fat cheddar
2	teaspoons	thyme
2	tablespoons	diet margarine
5	cups	water

Directions

- Set out hash browns to thaw

- Wash celery, carrots, and green onions. Slice celery and onions crossways in thin slices. Grate carrots

- Put diet margarine in a nonstick Dutch oven. Add celery, onions and grated carrots and cook over medium heat, stirring until onions are translucent and the celery is wilting. 6 to 7 minutes

- Stir in hash browns and cook, stirring, another 3 to 4 minutes

- Stir in all other ingredients except cheese. Cover and simmer about 10 minutes--do not allow to boil

- Remove from heat stir in cheese until blended

- Makes 10 to 11 cups of soup, about 1 3/4 cups per serving. 205 calories per serving

CALORIES AS FAT | SODIUM | CHOLESTEROL | FAT Saturated Total | CARBOHYDRATES Refined Complex Sugars Carbohydrates | PROTEIN | DIETARY FIBER | FRUITS & VEGETABLES

Cheeseburger Soup*

6 servings

Ingredients list

1	pound	ground round * see note
3	medium	yellow onions
6	medium	Italian plum tomatoes
2	medium	carrots
3	stalks	celery
3	medium	baking potatoes (3 medium or 2 large)
1	can	cheese soup
2	cans	(12 ounces each) evaporated skim milk
1	tablespoon	Mrs. Dash® Seasoning
1	teaspoon	garlic powder
4	cups	water

*can substitute Pre-browned all vegetable protein crumbles for a vegetarian version (e.g. Green Giant Harvest Burgers®, prebrowned crumbles, 12 ounces, frozen)

Directions

- Boil potatoes, peel and dice into 1/4 inch pieces.

- Peel and grate carrots, slice celery thinly, chop tomatoes very coarsely

- In a large nonstick Dutch oven, brown meat over medium heat stirring constantly, with carrots, onions, celery, and Mrs. Dash® Seasoning. Cook until meat is brown and the vegetables just become tender, 6 to 7 minutes

- Stir in potatoes, 4 cups water, cheese soup, the evaporated skim milk, and the garlic powder

- Bring to a simmer, stirring frequently, until thickening 5 to 7 minutes

- Stir in tomatoes and ladle into bowls

- Makes about 12 cups of soup, 2 cups per serving. 385 calories per serving

CALORIES AS FAT   SODIUM   CHOLESTEROL   FAT Saturated Total   CARBOHYDRATES Refined Complex Sugars Carbohydrates   PROTEIN   DIETARY FIBER   FRUITS & VEGETABLES

The Doctor Cooks

Soups

Cher's California Champagne Shrimp Soup

6 servings

Ingredients list

1 1/2	cups	grapefruit juice (unsweetened)
1	bottle	inexpensive, dry, champagne
3	cups	water
2	small	fish Bouillon cubes, or 2 teaspoon crystals
1	pound	fresh green beans
3	medium	carrots
1	bunch	green onions
1/2	pound	shrimp, raw
1	cup	couscous, dry

Directions

- Wash vegetables. Trim ends off beans and onions. Peel carrots. Julienne green beans (1/8 inch by 1/8 inch by 1 1/2 inch strips) chop white parts of onions, chop carrots. (Slice green parts of onions crossways into 1/2 inch slices and reserve in refrigerator, for garnish)

- Mix water, grapefruit juice, all but 1 cup of champagne and bouillon cubes in a large kettle or Dutch oven. Add vegetables and simmer for 20 minutes until vegetables are tender crisp

- Meanwhile make couscous: Cook couscous according to package directions, using only 1 teaspoon margarine, no salt, and 1 cup of the champagne replacing 1 of the cups of water

- Pack 6 portions of cooked couscous into 1/3 cup rounded measure, and unmound upside down in warmed soup bowls

- Stir shrimp into simmering broth, and cook until just turning pink

- Ladle soup gently around couscous in warmed bowls and serve immediately

- Makes 8 cups of soup, about 1 1/3 cups per serving. 315 calories per serving

CALORIES AS FAT   SODIUM   CHOLESTEROL   FAT Saturated Total   CARBOHYDRATES Refined Complex Sugars Carbohydrates   PROTEIN   DIETARY FIBER   FRUITS & VEGETABLES

The Doctor Cooks

Soups

Chicken-Lentil Mulligatawny Soup

6 servings

Ingredients list

2		chicken thighs, skinless
2		chicken legs, skinless
1	stalk	celery, chopped medium fine
5	cups	water
1	cup	yellow lentils
2 1/2	cups	water
1	medium	yellow onion, chopped
1/4	teaspoon	red pepper flakes
1/2	teaspoon	ground ginger
1/2	teaspoon	cinnamon
1	tablespoon	curry powder
6	bunches	fresh mint, if available
1	teaspoon	salt

Directions

- Put chicken pieces in a medium saucepan with 1/2 teaspoon salt, the chopped celery and 4 cups water and cook, covered, until chicken is very tender and pulling away from bones, about 30 minutes

- At the same time, in another saucepan, add lentils to 2 1/2 cups water, add 1/2 teaspoon salt, 1 teaspoon of the curry powder, the chopped onions and cook, covered, until lentils are tender and much of the water is absorbed. Remove from heat, add 1 cup warm water and puree all but 1/3 cup of the mixture in a food processor

- Remove cooled chicken from bone, discarding bones keeping all chicken broth. Chop chicken very coarsely and add back to broth mixture

- Stir in lentils, both pureed and un-pureed and all the spices (except mint) bring to a simmer and simmer together 10 to 15 minutes. Serve garnished with mint sprigs

- Makes 7 to 8 cups, about 1 1/3 cups per serving. 205 calories per serving

| CALORIES AS FAT | SODIUM | CHOLESTEROL | FAT Saturated Total | CARBOHYDRATES Refined Complex Sugars Carbohydrates | PROTEIN | DIETARY FIBER | FRUITS & VEGETABLES |

Chicken Wild Rice Soup

6 servings

Ingredients list

3	tablespoons	Diet Margerine
3		large celery stalks
1		large carrot
1		clove garlic
2	medium	onions
2		chicken breasts without skin
1	pound	sliced mushrooms
2		bay leaves
1	teaspoon	freshly ground pepper
1	teaspoon	dried dill
1/2	teaspoon	curry powder
1/2	cup	wild rice
1/2	cup	raw brown rice
1/2	teaspoon	salt
1		egg substitute (equivalent to 2 eggs)
1	tablespoon	flour

Directions

- Bring 2 quarts water to boil, add chicken breasts, and 1/2 tsp salt, reduce heat and simmer, covered, 20 minutes
- Remove chicken from bones (if not boneless) skim broth, chop meat and reserve it
- Add both rices and all spices to liquid and continue to simmer
- Chop celery, carrots, onions and garlic
- In skillet melt 2 tablespoons diet margerine, add all chopped vegetables (onions, carrots, garlic and celery) and cook, over medium heat, until softened, stirring about five minutes
- Add vegetable mixture to broth rice mixture and simmer, covered, for 1 hour, adding more liquid if soup is too thick
- Remove soup from heat
- Melt 1 tablespoon diect margerine in a nonstick frying pan, stir sliced mushrooms, and stir, over medium heat 3 to 5 minutes, until just cooked. Stir in soup
- mix egg substitute with 1 tbsp flour

- Remove 1 cup of hot soup, and stir, with wire whisk, into egg substitute-flour mixture. Then pour all back into the pan and stir gently with wire whisk until thickening
- Stir in reserved chicken meat
- Heat soup gently without boiling and serve as soon as hot again.
- Makes about 9 to 10 cups soup, 1 1/2 cup per serving. 275 calories per serving

CALORIES AS FAT   SODIUM   CHOLESTEROL   FAT Saturated Total   CARBOHYDRATES Refined Complex Sugars Carbohydrates   PROTEIN   DIETARY FIBER   FRUITS & VEGETABLES

(Chicken Wild Rice Soup)

Chicken With 40 Cloves of Garlic Soup

6 servings

Ingredients list

4	heads	garlic
2	pounds	chicken breast halves without skin
1	teaspoon	salt
1	teaspoon	paprika
1	teaspoon	pepper
2	teaspoons	rosemary
2	teaspoons	basil
2	bunches	green onions
1/2	head	green cabbage
1	teaspoon	olive oil
2	ounces	angel hair pasta
6	cups	water
3	cups	dry white wine

Directions

- Wash onions then slice whites and green parts of onions separately, refrigerate greens
- Wash garlic heads, then trim off the pointed end of each to expose the cloves.
- Shred green cabbage into very thin slices, about 1 1/2 inches long. Set aside
- Mix spices and oil and rub onto both sides of chicken
- Place chicken in crock pot (if available) or nonstick Dutch oven with 3 cups of water and wine, and add garlic heads, white parts of onions (only), and cabbage to chicken and cook, over very low heat about 1 1/2 hours (or medium setting of crock pot, 3 to 4 hours) until chicken is tender and falling off bones, and garlic is soft and mushy
- Let cool slightly--remove bones and skin from chicken and cut into chunks. Skim all available fat from the soup
- Grasping each garlic head by the base (protect hand) squeeze until cloves of garlic squeeze out of their skins. Mash cloves gently and return to the soup, discarding the tough peel of the head.
- Cut up chicken and return to pot with vegetables. Add remaining water and broken pasta. Bring to a boil and simmer 12 to 15 minutes

- Stir in green parts of onions and ladle into bowls
- makes 12 cups of soup about 2 cups per serving 280 calories per serving

| CALORIES AS FAT | SODIUM | CHOLESTEROL | FAT Saturated Total | CARBOHYDRATES Refined Complex Sugars Carbohydrates | PROTEIN | DIETARY FIBER | FRUITS & VEGETABLES |

(Chicken With 40 Cloves of Garlic Soup)

The Doctor Cooks
Soups

Chinese Egg Drop Pea Pod Soup

6 servings

Ingredients list

1	package	(10 ounces) frozen baby peas
1	package	(10 ounces) frozen Chinese pea pods
6	cups	low sodium chicken broth
1	can	(8 ounces) sliced waterchestnuts
2		green onions, chopped
2		eggs, beaten lightly

Directions

- Bring broth to boil in large Dutch oven or soup kettle. Reduce heat to simmer. Stir in contents of both packages peas, and the waterchestnuts. Simmer 3 to 4 minutes

- Stir in chopped green onions and simmer 2 to 3 more minutes

- Remove from heat, stir in a swirling motion and pour beaten eggs in a ribbon into the swirling liquid

- Immediately ladle into heated bowls and serve

- Makes 8-9 cups of soup, 1 1/2 cups per serving. 98 calories per serving

CALORIES AS FAT   SODIUM   CHOLESTEROL   FAT Saturated Total   CARBOHYDRATES Refined Complex Sugars Carbohydrates   PROTEIN   DIETARY FIBER   FRUITS & VEGETABLES

Chinese Hot and Sour Tuna Soup

6 servings

Ingredients list

8	ounces	tuna steaks raw, coarsely chopped
1	can	(8 ounces) water chestnuts
2	cups	Chinese cabbage (Napa) thinly cross sliced
1	bunch	green onions
4	ounces	tofu
6		Chinese or Japanese dried mushrooms
1	tablespoon	fresh ginger, finely chopped
6	cups	low sodium chicken broth
1	teaspoon	sesame oil, if available
2	tablespoons	soy sauce lite
3	teaspoons	cornstarch
2	tablespoons	oil
1	teaspoon	fresh ground pepper
2	tablespoons	vinegar

Directions

- Slice tuna into thin ribbons. Stir together, gently, with 1 tablespoon soy sauce lite, 1 teaspoon cornstarch 1 tablespoon oil. When roughly mixed, place in refrigerator

- Slice water chestnuts into julienne. Slice whites and greens of green onions separately into 1 inch julienne

- Soak mushrooms until soft and cut in 1/8 inch slices

- In large wok or Dutch oven heat 1 tablespoon oil, then stir fry whites of onions, ginger, and mushrooms 1 to 2 minutes

- Add marinated tuna mixture to hot oil and stir fry, gently, until just turning white and opaque, remove from heat

- Stir in chicken broth and water chestnuts and return to heat and bring to a simmer, cook 7 minutes

- Stir in cabbage and simmer 2 more minutes

- Mix sesame oil with 2 teaspoon cornstarch and vinegar and pepper. Stir until smooth. Slowly stir into soup and simmer until thickening and clear

- Cut tofu into slivers and stir very gently into soup
- Ladle into heated bowls. Sprinkle with reserved chopped green onion to serve
- Makes 8 to 9 cups of soup 1 1/3 to 1 1/2 cups per serving. 150 calories per serving

CALORIES
AS FAT

SODIUM

CHOLESTEROL

FAT
Saturated Total

CARBOHYDRATES
Refined Complex
Sugars Carbohydrates

PROTEIN

DIETARY FIBER

FRUITS &
VEGETABLES

Country Captain Chicken Soup*

6 servings

Ingredients list

2		chicken thighs without skin, bone in
2		chicken breasts without skin, bone in
2	tablespoons	flour
1 1/2	teaspoons	white pepper
28	ounces	(2 cans) diced tomatoes in tomato juice
2	tablespoons	olive oil
2	medium	yellow onions
2	large	green peppers
2	medium	carrots
4		cloves garlic
1/2	teaspoon	salt
3	tablespoons	raisins
2	teaspoons	thyme
2	tablespoons	curry powder
1/2	cup	brown rice, raw
1/4	cup	cilantro, leaves
8	cups	water

Directions

- Cook chicken in a saucepan in 4 cups water and 1/2 teaspoon salt. When done let cool, reserve broth
- Using a slotted spoon, remove the chicken pieces onto a plate, strip from bones and chop into 3/4 inch chunks. Discard bones
- Peel and grate carrots, mince garlic, seed and coarsely chop green pepper. Peel and finely chop onions
- In a large nonstick Dutch oven, over medium heat, place 2 tablespoons oil
- Stir in garlic and chopped onions and cook, stirring, until translucent, about 4 to 5 minutes. Add green pepper and carrots then cook, stirring, 3 to 4 more minutes
- Stir in flour and cook 1 to 2 more minutes and remove from heat
- Stir in all other ingredients except cilantro and raisins (using broth from cooking the chicken and 4 additional cups of water)
- Simmer, covered, stirring occasionally for 45 minutes

- Put chicken pieces in the pot along with the raisins. Simmer 15 more minutes
- Ladle into 6 heated bowls and garnish with cilantro leaves
- Makes 12 cups, 2 cups per serving. 310 calories per serving

| CALORIES AS FAT | SODIUM | CHOLESTEROL | FAT Saturated Total | CARBOHYDRATES Refined Complex Sugars Carbohydrates | PROTEIN | DIETARY FIBER | FRUITS & VEGETABLES |

(Country Captain Chicken Soup)

Crab Gumbo Soup

6 servings*

Ingredients list

8	ounces	canned crabmeat, with liquid
2	8 oz. bottles	clam juice
3	medium	green peppers
1	pound	frozen okra
1	bunch	green onions (6 to 8 onions)
2	stalks	celery
3		cloves garlic
4	tablespoons	flour
3	tablespoons	olive oil
3		Granny Smith apples
6	cups	water
1/2	teaspoon	salt
1	teaspoon	paprika
1	teaspoon	thyme
1	teaspoon	dry mustard
1	teaspoon	ground cumin (or curry powder)
1/2	teaspoon	red pepper flakes (to taste, optional)
1/2	cup	raw brown (or white) rice

Directions

- Prepare vegetables: wash, then cut green onions crosswise into 1/4 inch slices, chop celery, seed and chop green peppers into 1/4 inch dice, mince garlic. Set out okra to thaw. Core, then chop apples, peel on

- Measure out spices and salt and mix together.

- Heat 2 tablespoons oil in a nonstick frying pan. Add flour and cook over medium heat, stirring with a wooden spoon, until the flour turns dark golden. (This takes time but is the secret to the final flavor.) Stir in spice mixture and cook, stirring, one more minute. Scrape mixture into soup kettle

- Without cleaning pan, add the remaining tablespoon oil and minced garlic, and cook, stirring, 1 to 2 minutes. Then add all the prepared vegetables, and add the frozen okra, and cook over medium heat, stirring frequently (mixture will be very dry) until vegetables are just beginning to show some browned area. (This takes 6 to 7 minutes) Add apple juice, and stir 1 to 2 more minutes, then scrape mixture into soup kettle with the flour spice mixture

- Add clam juice, water and rice to soup kettle. Simmer, covered, over low heat, approximately 30 minutes, until rice and vegetables are tender, and flavors are well mixed. Stir in crabmeat with its liquid during the last 3 to 4 minutes of cooking

- Makes about 12 cups soup, 2 cups per serving. Freezes and reheats well. 270 calories per serving

CALORIES
AS FAT

SODIUM

CHOLESTEROL

FAT
Saturated Total

CARBOHYDRATES
Refined Complex
Sugars Carbohydrates

PROTEIN

DIETARY FIBER

FRUITS &
VEGETABLES

(Crab Gumbo Soup)

Cranberry Fruit Soup

Serves six

Ingredients list

1/2	cup	frozen orange juice concentrate
1	quart	cranberry juice cocktail
1		lemon
12	ounces	fresh cranberries, or frozen
1	cup	sugar
3	cups	red wine (merlot or Chianti)
1	tablespoon	cornstarch
1/3	teaspoon	nutmeg
1/2	cup	nonfat sour cream

Directions

- Grate the lemon rind, producing 2 teaspoons finely grated rind and put it in a small bowl. Add to it the juice of the lemon and the orange juice concentrate and set aside

- Boil the cranberries in 2 cups cranberry juice 2 cups wine (with the cup of sugar mixed in) until tender, 10 minutes

- Puree cranberry

- Add processed cranberries back into sauce pan add juice of the lemon, lemon rind, nutmeg, frozen orange juice concentrate, the remaining wine, and the remaining cranberry juice. Bring just to simmer

- Dissolve cornstarch in a small amount of water, and stir slowly into the simmering soup, continuing to simmer, stirring until soup is thickening and clear

- Chill thoroughly--serve in chilled bowls, floating a generous tablespoon of sour cream in center

- Makes 8 cups of soup, 1 1/3 cups per serving. 400 calories per serving

| CALORIES ASFG | SODIUM | CHOLESTEROL | FAT Saturated Total | CARBOHYDRATES Refined Complex Sugars Carbohydrates | PROTEIN | DIETARY FIBER | FRUITS & VEGETABLES |

Creamy Vegetable Chowder
6 servings

Ingredients list

3	medium	yellow squash
3	medium	zucchini
1	pound	fresh mushrooms
1	large	bell pepper
1	bunch	green onions
1		lemon juice and rind
1	package	(10 ounces) frozen corn
1/3	cup	unsalted butter
3	teaspoons	vegetarian bouillon, or chicken bouillon granules
5	cups	water
2	cans	(25 ounces) evaporated skim milk
1	teaspoon	fresh ground black pepper

Directions

- Wash and chop green onions. Finely grate 1 teaspoon lemon rind and squeeze the juice. Wash and cut the zucchini and the yellow squash in half longways, then crossways into 1/4 inch slices. Wash mushrooms and slice thickly. Seed then cut red bell pepper into approximately 1/2 inch by 3/4 inch strips. Put corn out to thaw

- If you have microwave, place the squash and red bell pepper slices in a glass dish, add 1 cup of water, cover with clear microwavable wrap and cook on high 5 minutes until softening. (If no microwave, steam 7 to 10 minutes in 1 cup of water.) In each case save all liquid

- In a large Dutch oven, melt butter, over low heat. Add the lemon rind and pepper

- Add chopped green onions and mushrooms and cook together 5 to 7 minutes over low heat, stirring occasionally and avoiding browning

- Stir in juice from cooking vegetables, four additional cups of water, bouillon and lemon juice. Add corn

- Simmer , covered, over low heat 10 to 12 minutes, until vegetables are tender and the flavors well blended

- Remove from heat and stir in the two cans of evaporated skim milk

- Return to low heat and cook, watching and stirring occasionally, until small bubbles just start to break the surface around the edge. Do not allow to boil because it may curdle

- Serve immediately by ladling into heated bowls, dividing vegetables evenly
- Makes 10 to 11 cups of soup, 1 2/3 to 2 cups per serving. 280 calories per serving

CALORIES
AS FAT

SODIUM

CHOLESTEROL

FAT
Saturated Total

CARBOHYDRATES
Refined Complex
Sugars Carbohydrates

PROTEIN

DIETARY FIBER

FRUITS &
VEGETABLES

Cuban Chicken Rice Soup

6 servings

Ingredients list

4		cloves garlic
3		boneless chicken breasts without skin
2	tablespoons	olive oil
2	large	yellow onions
6	ounces	(1 can) tomato paste
1	cup	white rice, raw
6	large	black olives, pitted and sliced
3		bay leaves
8	cups	water
10	ounces	(1 box) small frozen peas
1	teaspoon	salt

Directions

- Chop onions and garlic together medium fine. Cut chicken in 1 inch by 1/2 inch chunks
- Heat oil in a Dutch oven. Add onions and garlic and cook, stirring, until translucent 4 to 5 minutes
- Stir in chicken and cook, stirring, until just browning 6 to 7 minutes
- Stir in olives, rice, bay leaves, tomato paste, salt and water
- Simmer, covered, over low heat about 45 minutes, until the rice is done
- Stir in thawed peas and black olives and ladle into bowls
- Makes 9 to 10 cups soup, 1 1/2 cups per serving, 360 calories

| CALORIES AS FAT | SODIUM | CHOLESTEROL | FAT Saturated Total | CARBOHYDRATES Refined Complex Sugars Carbohydrates | PROTEIN | DIETARY FIBER | FRUITS & VEGETABLES |

Cucumber Dill Soup

6 servings

Ingredients list

3	large	cucumbers
1/2	bunch	green onions
1	quart	buttermilk
1	cup	nonfat sour cream
1	cup	water
2	teaspoons	dill
2	teaspoons	sugar
1/2	teaspoon	salt
2	teaspoons	lemon juice

Directions

- Mince white parts of green onions fine. Slice green parts.

- Cut cucumbers in half and core out seeds, coarsely grate cucumbers

- Stir all ingredients together thoroughly. Refrigerate until cold

- Makes 7 to 8 cups of soup, 1 1/4 per serving. 140 calories per serving

CALORIES AS FAT   SODIUM   CHOLESTEROL   FAT Saturated Total   CARBOHYDRATES Refined Complex Sugars Carbohydrates   PROTEIN   DIETARY FIBER   FRUITS & VEGETABLES

Curried Chicken Cheese Soup

Serves six

Ingredients list

2		chicken breasts without skin
6		Italian plum tomatoes
1	bunch	green onions
1		yellow onion quartered
2		carrots diced
2		celery stalks including tops
2		bay leaves
1	tablespoon	curry powder
1/2	teaspoon	allspice
1	can	(12 1/2 ounces) evaporated skim milk
1/2	cup	shredded lowfat cheddar cheese
1	teaspoon	salt
1	teaspoon	fresh ground pepper
1	tablespoon	flour

Directions

- In large saucepan gently boil chicken breasts with 4 cups water, salt, pepper, bay leaves, celery tops (only), 1 onion quartered, covered, for about 1/2 hour

- Save this broth--Discard celery tops, bay leaves, onion. Remove chicken from bones, discarding bones, and cut chicken into 1/2 inch cubes, reserve

- Peel and chop carrots, slice celery ribs thinly and add to broth. Slice the green onions, reserve the green parts and add white parts to broth

- Simmer covered, stirring occasionally 1/2 hour until vegetables softening

- Chop and seed tomatoes

- Add curry powder, and allspice to pot

- Mix the flour into the milk until smooth. Stir milk mixture slowly into simmering soup and cook over low heat, stirring 2 minutes until thick

- Remove from heat and stir in cheese until smooth

- Stir in tomatoes, and reserved chopped chicken, and bring just to simmer
- To serve, sprinkle green onions liberally over each bowl of soup
- Makes about 8 cups of soup, 1 1/3 cups per serving. 225 calories per serving.

CALORIES AS FAT   SODIUM   CHOLESTEROL   FAT
Saturated Total   CARBOHYDRATES
Refined Complex
Sugars Carbohydrates   PROTEIN   DIETARY FIBER   FRUITS & VEGETABLES

Czechoslovakian Pork Goulash Soup*

6 servings

Ingredients list

1	pound	pork tenderloin, trimmed
1	bunch	green onions
5	medium	red potatoes
4	medium	Italian plum tomatoes
3	medium	carrots
4		cloves garlic
1/2	pound	mushrooms
1	can	(8 ounces) sauerkraut
6	cups	water
2	cups	white wine
1	teaspoon	paprika
1	teaspoon	white pepper
1	teaspoon	caraway seed
4	tablespoons	flour
1	cup	nonfat sour cream
2	tablespoons	vegetable oil

Directions

- Trim tenderloin of all fat. Cut into 1/2 inch cubes
- Mix 2 tablespoons of the flour with the paprika and the pepper in a sealable plastic bag. Drop in pork cubes and shake until all flour is absorbed onto the meat. Refrigerate while preparing other ingredients
- Chop onions and garlic fine. Wash and cut the red potatoes into eighths, peeling intact. Wash and chop tomatoes medium fine, removing seeds. Peel and chop carrots medium fine. Chop mushrooms
- Add the 2 tablespoons of oil to a large Dutch oven. Cook onions, garlic and carrots together, stirring, until onions are translucent, 3 to 4 minutes
- Add tomatoes and mushrooms and cook, stirring, 3 to 4 more minutes. Add meat and cook another 7 to 10 minutes
- Add white wine, sauerkraut, with its liquid, water, and potatoes. Simmer, covered, over low heat until the potatoes are just fork tender, about 30 minutes

- Mix remaining 2 tablespoons of flour in 1/2 cup water and add for the last 5 minutes of cooking
- Remove from heat, swirl in sour cream and caraway seeds and ladle into bowls
- Makes about 10 cups, 1 2/3 cups per serving. 380 calories

CALORIES AS FAT SODIUM CHOLESTEROL FAT Saturated Total CARBOHYDRATES Refined Complex Sugars Carbohydrates PROTEIN DIETARY FIBER FRUITS & VEGETABLES

100% 50% 0%

(Czechoslovakian Pork Goulash Soup)

Easy Shrimp Bisque
Serves six

Ingredients list

2	packages	(6 ounces each) frozen cooked salad shrimp
2	tablespoons	diet margarine
4	tablespoons	flour
2	medium	onions
1		clove garlic
1	teaspoon	paprika
1/8	teaspoon	cayenne pepper
3	cups	skim milk
1	can	evaporated skim milk
1/2	cup	dry sherry
1/3	cup	nonfat sour cream

Directions

- Chop onions and garlic together until very fine
- Reserve 12 small shrimp, then chop the remaining frozen shrimp medium fine, placing in a bowl to catch all liquid while thawing
- Melt diet margarine in heavy bottom sauce pan, over medium low heat
- Cook onions and garlic until translucent, stirring constantly. Do not let brown. Stir in flour, paprika, and cayenne pepper, and cook, stirring, for 30 seconds--will be very dry
- Add milk slowly, along with any liquid shrimp has released while chopping and thawing, and cook, stirring continuously until mixture thickens and comes to a boil
- Stir in sherry and chopped shrimp, remove from heat
- Top with 1 tablespoon nonfat sour cream and 2 reserved shrimp, per serving to garnish
- Makes about 6 cups, at 1 cup per serving. 235 calories per serving

CALORIES
AS FAT

SODIUM

CHOLESTEROL

FAT
Saturated   Total

CARBOHYDRATES
Refined   Complex
Sugars   Carbohydrates

PROTEIN

DIETARY FIBER

FRUITS &
VEGETABLES

Flemish Beef Stew*

6 servings

Ingredients list

2	pounds	lean boneless chuck roast
8	ounces	(1 package) thawed frozen peas
6	medium	yellow onions
1	tablespoon	vegetable oil
1	tablespoon	diet margarine
2	tablespoons	cider vinegar
24	ounces	beer (2 bottles)
1	teaspoon	salt
2	teaspoons	sugar
1	tablespoon	thyme
3		bay leaves
2	tablespoons	flour
1 1/2	teaspoons	ground pepper
1	pound	sliced mushrooms
6	medium	Italian tomatoes, cut in quarters
6	cups	water

Directions

- Trim beef and cut in 1/2 inch by 1/2 inch by 1 inch strips
- Mix 1/2 teaspoon salt, flour and 1 teaspoon of the thyme in a closable plastic bag. Add cut up meat and shake until entire flour mixture is absorbed. Set bag aside in refrigerator
- Peel and slice onions. Melt the tablespoon of diet margarine in a nonstick 2 1/2 to 3 quart Dutch oven over medium heat.
- Add onions, cook, stirring frequently, until onions turn brown and almost mushy
- Stir in sugar and cook several more minutes. Remove onions to plate and keep warm
- Using same pan, add oil. Add floured meat and cook over medium high heat, stirring occasionally, until nicely browned on all sides
- Add back onions, and stir in all other ingredients except frozen peas--set them out to thaw
- Bring to a simmer. Simmer covered for 1 1/2 hours. Replacing liquid as needed, until it becomes a rich brown broth and the meat becomes very tender

- Divide thawed peas between bowls. Ladle in beef stew, dividing evenly between bowls

- Makes about 9 cups of soup, 1 1/2 cups per serving. 550 calories per serving.

100% 50% 0% CALORIES AS FAT   SODIUM   CHOLESTEROL   FAT Saturated Total   CARBOHYDRATES Refined Complex Sugars Carbohydrates   PROTEIN   DIETARY FIBER   FRUITS & VEGETABLES

(Flemish Beef Stew)

French Peasant Soup

Serves 6

Ingredients

1	envelope	low sodium onion soup mix *see note
1	can	(16 ounces) baked beans (w/ tomato, not molasses style)
3		garlic cloves
6	cups	water
3	cups	thinly shredded cabbage
2	teaspoons	marjoram

*1 1/2 ounces e.g. Bordens® or Mrs. Grass®

Directions

- Mince garlic
- Mix all ingredients in a nonstick Dutch oven, cover and simmer together 1/2 hour over low heat, stirring occasionally to prevent sticking or burning
- Makes 7 to 8 cups of soup, about 1 1/3 cups per serving. 100 calories per serving

| CALORIES AS FAT | SODIUM | CHOLESTEROL | FAT Saturated Total | CARBOHYDRATES Refined Complex Sugars Carbohydrates | PROTEIN | DIETARY FIBER | FRUITS & VEGETABLES |

Fresh Tomato Soup

6 servings

Ingredients list

6	medium	Italian plum tomatoes
2		cloves garlic
1	can	(11 1/2 ounces) tomato juice
1	tablespoon	balsamic vinegar
2	tablespoons	Diet margerine
1/4	teaspoon	salt
1/2	teaspoon	fresh ground pepper
2	slices	wheat bread or white
6	teaspoons	feta cheese (optional)

Directions

- Cut bread into crouton size pieces and toast in low oven until dry

- Cut tomatoes into quarters, remove seeds on paper towel and put into blender with all other ingredients except croutons and feta cheese

- Blend until smooth. Serve at room temperature, or chilled topped with croutons and a sprinkle of feta cheese

- Makes 6 to 7 cups of soup, about 1 cup per serving. 100 calories per serving

CALORIES AS FAT   SODIUM   CHOLESTEROL   FAT Saturated Total   CARBOHYDRATES Refined Complex Sugars Carbohydrates   PROTEIN   DIETARY FIBER   FRUITS & VEGETABLES

Fruit Soup

6 servings

Ingredients list

1	quart	white grape juice
2	cups	red wine
1	cup	water
2	teaspoons	cornstarch
1	pint	fresh blueberries
1	cup	sliced fresh nectarines or peaches

Directions

- Mix juice and wine in a large saucepan and start heating over medium heat
- Stir cornstarch into water until smooth and add to saucepan
- Bring to a simmer, and simmer for 5 minutes, stirring frequently, until slightly thickened
- Remove from heat and let cool, then stir in fresh fruit and chill until cold
- Makes 7 to 8 cups of soup, 1 1/4 cup per serving. 200 calories per serving

CALORIES AS FAT   SODIUM   CHOLESTEROL   FAT Saturated Total   CARBOHYDRATES Refined Complex Sugars Carbohydrates   PROTEIN   DIETARY FIBER   FRUITS & VEGETABLES

Georgia Brunswick Stew

6 servings

Ingredients list

2		boneless chicken breasts without skin
8	ounces	2 pork chops, bone in
1	bunch	green onions
6	small	red potatoes
1	box	(10 ounces) frozen baby lima beans
10	ounces	(10 ounces) frozen corn kernels
3/4	cup	catsup
2		lemon
3/4	teaspoon	salt
9	cups	water

Directions

- Cut red potatoes in half. Boil in several cups of water until just fork tender. Drain and reserve

- Place 6 cups of water in a Dutch oven, or soup kettle. Stir in salt and catsup. Add the chicken breasts and the pork chops (trimmed of all visible fat)

- Cut lemon in half, squeeze the juice and reserve, add both squeezed halves to the soup kettle

- Simmer, covered over medium low heat, about 1 hour, until pork falls from bones and the chicken is beginning to flake

- Remove meat and place on a plate to cool slightly, keeping liquid in the pot. Discard bones and shred meat with fingers. Add shredded meat back into the simmering pot

- Add the corn, lima beans, cooked potatoes, chopped green onions, lemon juice and the rest of the water to the pot and cook 15 to 20 minutes until the vegetables are tender and flavors are well blended

- Makes 10 to 11 cups soup, 1 2/3 cups per serving, 350 calories per serving

CALORIES AS FAT   SODIUM   CHOLESTEROL   FAT Saturated Total   CARBOHYDRATES Refined Complex Sugars Carbohydrates   PROTEIN   DIETARY FIBER   FRUITS & VEGETABLES

German Omelet Consommé

6 servings

Ingredients list

1	can	(10 3/4 ounces) beef consommé diluted with 2 1/2 cans water
2		egg substitute, equivalent to 2 eggs each
4	slices	ham extra lean, sandwich style
1	tablespoon	diet margarine
1	bunch	green onions, finely chopped
1	tablespoon	flour
1	bunch	parsely
1/2	teaspoon	pepper
		nonstick cooking spray

Directions

- Chop green onions and parsely finely, cut ham into 1/2 inch by 1/2 inch squares

- Spray 8 inch square baking pan with nonstick spray. Begin heating oven to 350 degrees

- In small frying pan cook finely chopped onion with tablespoon of diet margarine, until white just turning translucent

- Add squares (1/2 by 1/2 inch) ham and continue cooking, stirring constantly, until just browning

- Add the tablespoon flour, and continue to cook, stirring, briefly until flour absorbed, remove from heat

- Beat Egg Beaters® 99% egg substitute with mixer until just frothing. Stir in cooked ham and vegetable mixture, stir in chopped parsely

- Pour egg mixture into prepared pan. Bake 20 minutes, or until top springs back when touched with finger tip.

- Cool and cut into 1 1/2 inch squares (about 25). Place in 6 warmed small bowls, about 4 squares per bowl. Cover with about 3/4 cup consommé per serving

- Makes about 6 cups of soup, 1 cup per serving. 60 calories per serving

CALORIES
AS FAT

SODIUM

CHOLESTEROL

FAT
Saturated Total

CARBOHYDRATES
Refined Complex
Sugars Carbohydrates

PROTEIN

DIETARY FIBER

FRUITS &
VEGETABLES

Green Chili Egg Drop Soup

6 servings

Ingredients list

2	cans	whole green chili peppers, mild or medium as desired
3		chicken breast halves without skin (about 6 ounces each)
1/2	bunch	green onions, chopped
1	teaspoon	salt
2		eggs
6	cups	water

Directions

- Place the skinned chicken breasts in large saucepan with 6 cups of water and 1 teaspoon salt

- Simmer, covered, until firm and white, but still tender

- Remove breasts and chop into 1/2 inch cubes

- Skim fat and other residual from top of cooking liquid

- Return chicken to liquid, add green onions, and drained canned sliced chilies

- Bring to boil then simmer for about 5 minutes to blend flavors

- Beat eggs together in a cup.

- Remove soup from heat, stir until swirling, and pour eggs into soup in a thin stream, continuing to stir in a gently swirling motion

- Ladle into heated bowls. Makes about 7 1/2 cups of soup, 1 1/4 cup per serving. 100 calories per serving

CALORIES AS FAT   SODIUM   CHOLESTEROL   FAT Saturated Total   CARBOHYDRATES Refined Complex Sugars Carbohydrates   PROTEIN   DIETARY FIBER   FRUITS & VEGETABLES

Honeydew Melon Soup
6 servings

Ingredients list

1	large	ripe honeydew melon (3 to 4 pounds)
7		ripe kiwi fruit
3	tablespoons	honey
1		lime, juice only
1/2	cup	nonfat sour cream

Directions

- Peel and seed chilled honeydew melon, then cut into chunks and place in a food processor container. Pour lime juice and honey over, then blend.

- Peel kiwi fruit. Cut 6 fruit into chunks and add to blender. (Slice remaining kiwi into 6 slices for garnish)

- Blend until smooth. Divide into 6 chilled bowls. Garnish with a generous tablespoon of sour cream and a slice of kiwi fruit

- Makes 6 to 7 cups of soup, 1 cup per serving. 140 calories per serving

CALORIES AS FAT   SODIUM   CHOLESTEROL   FAT Saturated Total   CARBOHYDRATES Refined Complex Sugars Carbohydrates   PROTEIN   DIETARY FIBER   FRUITS & VEGETABLES

Indian Tomato Rasam Soup

6 servings

Ingredients list

1 1/2	cups	dried lentils
6	cups	water
6	medium	Italian plum tomatoes
4		cloves garlic, finely minced
1	cup	fresh coriander leaves, coarsely chopped
1	tablespoon	olive oil
1/2	teaspoon	salt
1	teaspoon	chili powder
1	tablespoon	curry powder
2	teaspoons	mustard seeds
1/2	teaspoon	crushed red pepper
4	tablespoons	lemon juice
1	teaspoon	black pepper
1	tablespoon	flour
1/3	cup	nonfat yogurt

Directions

- Mince garlic
- Add Lentils to 3 cups of water and stir in 1/2 of the garlic, the salt, and the tablespoon of curry powder. Then simmer, covered in a medium saucepan 25 to 30 minutes until softening and most of the liquid is absorbed. Let cool slightly.
- Process lentil mixture in a blender or food processor
- Chop tomatoes, about 1/4 inch dice, removing most of the seeds as you go
- To a soup kettle or Dutch oven add: the remaining 3 cups of water, chili powder, black pepper, the pureed lentils and the tomatoes. Simmer 15 to 20 minutes, stirring occasionally
- Put oil in a small frying pan. Add the remaining minced garlic and cook until just starting to brown. Add mustard seeds and cook, stirring until they just start to pop--stir in flour, then add all at once to hot soup
- Bring to a simmer and cook, stirring, until slightly thickened
- Stir in lemon juice
- Give a brisk stir just before ladling into 6 bowls. Place 1 tablespoon yogurt on top of each bowl and sprinkle the surface of the soup very liberally with chopped fresh coriander leaves

- Makes about 9 cups, 1 1/2 cups per serving. 230 calories per serving

CALORIES
AS FAT

SODIUM

CHOLESTEROL

FAT
Saturated   Total

CARBOHYDRATES
Refined Complex
Sugars Carbohydrates

PROTEIN

DIETARY FIBER

FRUITS &
VEGETABLES

(Indian Tomato Rasam Soup)

Italian White Bean Soup
6 servings

Ingredients list

2	cans	(16 ounces each) white beans, with liquid
1	bunch	green onions
4	medium	carrots
3	stalks	celery w/leaves
4		cloves garlic, minced
3	medium	Italian plum tomatoes
6	cups	water
2	tablespoons	olive oil
1/2	teaspoon	rosemary
1 1/2	teaspoons	basil
1/2	teaspoon	thyme
1/4	teaspoon	oregano
1/2	teaspoon	salt
1/2	teaspoon	ground black pepper
2		bay leaves
1/4	teaspoon	crushed red pepper
1/2	cup	pasta (any small pasta) uncooked

Directions

- Chop green onions into 1/2 inch lengths, peel and dice carrot, chop celery. Mince garlic, coarsely chop tomatoes removing seeds.

- Heat olive oil in large Dutch oven, over medium heat. Add garlic, chopped green onions, carrots and celery and cook, stirring, about 5 minutes

- Remove from heat and stir in liquid from both cans of beans, and beans from one can, reserving the beans from the second can

- Add salt, water, spices and tomatoes

- Reduce heat to simmer, cover, and cook 30 minutes, stirring occasionally, until carrots and celery are tender and flavors blended

- Add the pasta, then cover and simmer another 10 minutes, stirring occasionally, until pasta just softening

- Mash remaining drained can of beans coarsely with a potato masher or back of large spoon and stir into soup. Bring back to a boil, then reduce heat and simmer for 5 more minutes
- Makes 9 to 10 cups, 1 1/2 cups per serving. 300 calories per serving

| CALORIES AS FAT | SODIUM | CHOLESTEROL | FAT Saturated Total | CARBOHYDRATES Refined Complex Sugars Carbohydrates | PROTEIN | DIETARY FIBER | FRUITS & VEGETABLES |

(Italian White Bean Soup)

Italian Beef Soup with Two Peppers*

6 servings

Ingredients list

8	ounces	pepperoncini peppers (1 jar w/liquid)
1 1/2	pounds	boneless chuck steak, lean and trimmed, cut in large chunks
1	medium	yellow onion
1	bunch	green onions
2	cloves	garlic
3	medium	green peppers
2	medium	carrots
1	can	(10 1/2 ounces) beef bouillon
2	teaspoons	oregano
2	teaspoons	basil
1/2	teaspoon	rosemary, crushed
4	cups	water

Directions

- Mince garlic, rinse and coarsely chop green onions, cut yellow onion vertically into 1/16th wedges, wash and seed green peppers and cut in 1 inch by 1 inch chunks
- Chop carrots medium fine
- Put all ingredients in a crock pot, seal top with aluminum foil and put cover on
- Cook on low about 6 hours, until meat is falling apart
- Remove meat to platter and shred in bitesize pieces. Return to soup and serve
- Makes about 9 cups of soup, 1 1/2 cups per serving. 488 calories per serving

CALORIES AS FAT   SODIUM   CHOLESTEROL   FAT Saturated Total   CARBOHYDRATES Refined Complex Sugars Carbohydrates   PROTEIN   DIETARY FIBER   FRUITS & VEGETABLES

Italian Fish Soup (Cioppino)*

6 servings

Ingredients list

3	pounds	sea bass, boned skinned and cut into 1 1/2 inch chunks
16	ounces	clam juice (2 eight ounce bottles)
2	medium	onions
1		leek (white part only)
1	stalk	celery w/leaves
1		bay leaf
1/2	teaspoon	thyme
1/2	teaspoon	fennel seeds
4		cloves garlic
8	ounces	scallops
12	small	clams (scrubbed)
1	cup	white wine
1	tablespoon	vegetable oil
1/2	teaspoon	salt
1/2	teaspoon	fresh ground pepper
1/4	teaspoon	saffron (optional)
6	thick pieces	Italian bread
6		Italian tomatoes, chopped into coarse chunks, seeds removed
4	cups	water

Directions

- Place clam juice in kettle along with 4 cups water, salt, one chopped medium onion, chopped leek, celery, bay leaf, pepper, thyme, fennel. Heat to boiling, then simmer covered for 20 minutes, making a broth

- Add saffron, if using

- Chop the remaining onion finely, mince the garlic. Heat vegetable oil in Dutch oven, and cook onion and garlic in oil, stirring until tender, 3 to 4 minutes

- Add sea bass and brown lightly. Add in vegetable broth from step 1 above. Add tomatoes, wine, clams, and scallops.   Heat to boiling, cover and simmer until fish is cooked through, and clams have opened (discard any which do not open) approximately 10 to 15 minutes

- Serve in heated bowls with a thick slice of Italian bread floated in the center of each serving

- Makes about 10 to 11 cups of soup, 1 3/4 to 2 cups per serving. 490 calories per serving

CALORIES
AS FAT   SODIUM   CHOLESTEROL   FAT
                            Saturated Total

CARBOHYDRATES
Refined   Complex
Sugars   Carbohydrates   PROTEIN   DIETARY FIBER   FRUITS &
VEGETABLES

(Italian Fish Soup Cioppino)

Italian Minestrone*

6 servings

Ingredients list

4		cloves garlic
1	bunch	(6 to 8) green onions
25	slices	turkey pepperoni
3	medium	carrots
8	medium	Italian plum tomatoes
2	stalks	celery
13	ounces	Italian green beans, with liquid
8	ounces	chickpeas, canned, with liquid
8	ounces	kidney beans, canned, with liquid
1/4	cup	cilantro, coarsely chopped
1		lime
1/2	teaspoon	basil
1/2	teaspoon	oregano
1/2	teaspoon	rosemary
1	tablespoon	olive oil
6	cups	water
1/2	cup	small shell pasta
1	tablespoon	shredded Parmesan cheese

Directions

- Prepare vegetables: chop garlic finely, chop green onions in 1/2 inch pieces, peel and chop carrots, chop celery
- Finely grate 1 teaspoon of the lime peel. Squeeze juice and reserve separately
- Chop pepperoni very coarsely
- Chop tomatoes coarsely
- Heat oil in a large Dutch oven, stir in garlic and onions, cook 2 to 3 minutes.
- Stir in chopped carrots and celery, cook 3 to 4 minutes, stirring occasionally. Stir in pepperoni. Stir in tomatoes, cook 2 to 3 minutes
- Stir in water, spices, chickpeas, kidney beans, Italian green beans (adding the liquid from all three beans), cilantro, and grated lime. Cover and simmer 15 minutes, stirring occasionally
- Stir in pasta and simmer an additional 15 minutes

- Stir in lime juice. Ladle into heated soup bowls and serve, topped with Parmesan cheese
- Makes about 10 cups soup, 1 2/3 cups per serving. 310 calories per serving

CALORIES AS FAT   SODIUM   CHOLESTEROL   FAT Saturated Total   CARBOHYDRATES Refined Complex Sugars Carbohydrates   PROTEIN   DIETARY FIBER   FRUITS & VEGETABLES

(Italian Minestrone)

Italian Ossobucho (Veal Shank) Soup*

6 servings

Ingredients list

3	pounds	veal shank, meaty, cut by butcher into 1 inch pieces, bone in
1	cup	uncooked Orzo pasta
2	tablespoons	olive oil
1	teaspoon	fresh ground pepper
2	tablespoons	flour
1/2	teaspoon	salt
2	teaspoons	vegetable bouillon (2 cubes)
7	cups	water
1	tablespoon	Basil
2	teaspoons	thyme
6	medium	Italian plum tomatoes coarsely chopped
6	large	cloves garlic
1	cup	fresh parsley, finely chopped
1		lemon, juice, and 1/2 finely grated lemon zest

Directions

- Mix salt, pepper flour and basil together and rub over the veal shank pieces

- Heat olive oil in large Dutch oven. Brown veal pieces thoroughly, removing to heated plate, as needed for space

- Return all veal to pan. Add bouillon and 7 cups water. Simmer, covered for 1 hour, until fork tender. In the mean time, make the "gremolata"--Chop garlic and parsley together until fine. Stir in the lemon juice and zest. This is the gremolata

- Add Orzo, thyme and tomatoes to soup and simmer, covered, another 20 minutes or so until Orzo is cooked and soft. Remove from heat

- Ladle hot soup into 6 bowls, dividing Orzo and veal pieces evenly. Divide the Gremolata mixture into 6 portions and sprinkle over the top of each bowl

- Makes about 9 cups of soup, 1 1/2 cups per serving. 380 calories per serving

CALORIES AS FAT   SODIUM   CHOLESTEROL   FAT Saturated Total   CARBOHYDRATES Refined Complex Sugars Carbohydrates   PROTEIN   DIETARY FIBER   FRUITS & VEGETABLES

Japanese Buckwheat-Noodle Soup

6 servings

Ingredients list

6	cups	low sodium chicken broth
1	bunch	green onions
2	tablespoons	soy sauce (lite)
1/2	teaspoon	sugar
6	slices	fresh ginger (1/8 inch thick)
4	ounces	buckwheat noodles
1/4	pound	Chinese cabbage, thinly sliced
3		Chinese radishes, thinly sliced

Directions

- Chop whites of onions, sliver green portions 1 to 2 inches long

- Bring chicken broth to a boil. Add white parts of onions and the slices of ginger. Simmer 7 to 10 minutes while cooking noodles (see last step)

- Arrange 6 bowls--divide the thin slices of cabbage, the very thin slices of radishes, and the green parts of the onions into 6 bowls. Set aside

- Break noodles into 2 to 3 inch lengths. Cook noodles in boiling water until done, then drain and divide between the 6 bowls. Remove ginger slices from hot broth. Pour hot broth into prepared bowls and serve

- Makes 6 cups of soup, 1 cup per serving. 116 calories per serving

CALORIES AS FAT   SODIUM   CHOLESTEROL   FAT Saturated Total   CARBOHYDRATES Refined Complex Sugars Carbohydrates   PROTEIN   DIETARY FIBER   FRUITS & VEGETABLES

Jellied Madrilène Gazpacho

6 servings

Ingredients list

2	envelopes	unflavored gelatin
2	cans	(12 ounces each) diet 7up
2	cans	(10 ounces each) consommé
1	large	lemon *see note
3		Italian tomatoes
1	tablespoon	Worcestershire Sauce
1		green pepper, chopped fine
1/2	bunch	green onions
1	stalk	celery, w/leaves

*1/2, use the juice only, then cut the other 1/2 of the lemon into 6 wedges

Directions

- Soften gelatin in consommé; then heat, stirring constantly until gelatin dissolves
- Remove from heat and stir in lemon juice, Worcestershire sauce and 7up
- Pour into 9 inch by 9 inch pan and chill. When firm, cut into 1/2 inch cubes
- Chop vegetables together. Divide cubes and chopped vegetables between 6 chilled glasses, garnish with lemon wedges and serve
- 70 calories per serving

Lasagna Soup*

6 servings

Ingredients list

1	cup	cottage cheese, 2% fat
1	package	frozen chopped spinach
1		egg
1/4	cup	flour
4	tablespoons	Parmesan cheese, shredded
26	ounces	(1 jar) Reduced fat spaghetti sauce
5	cups	water
4		lasagna noodles
1	teaspoon	basil
1	teaspoon	thyme
		nonstick spray

Directions

- Thaw spinach and pat dry on paper towels

- Break lasagna noodles in half and cook in boiling water until just tender (12 to 15 minutes) then drain and cut into 1 inch squares

- Heat oven to 350 degrees, spray an 8 inch square pan with nonstick pan spray

- In blender or food processor, mix cottage cheese with 3 tablespoons of the Parmesan cheese

- Stir in egg and flour, and blend briefly, then add chopped spinach and blend only until mixed. Pour into prepared pan and bake 25 minutes, until firm

- In soup kettle or Dutch oven, mix spaghetti sauce, water, basil and thyme, and bring to a simmer

- Stir in cooked noodles and simmer for 3 to 5 minutes

- Cut cooked spinach mixture into squares, 6 by 6 (making 36 squares) put 6 squares each in 6 warmed soup bowls

- Ladle in the hot soup, dividing noodles evenly between bowls. Sprinkle with remaining Parmesan cheese

- Makes about 10 cups soup, 1 2/3 cup per serving. 348 calories per serving

CALORIES AS FAT   SODIUM   CHOLESTEROL   FAT Saturated Total   CARBOHYDRATES Refined Complex Sugars Carbohydrates   PROTEIN   DIETARY FIBER   FRUITS & VEGETABLES

Margarita Shrimp Soup

6 servings

Ingredients list

1	pound	medium shrimp, peeled and deveined
4	large	cloves garlic
1	bunch	green onions
1/2	tablespoon	lime zest, finely grated
1	tablespoon	orange zest, finely grated
1	teaspoon	hot pepper sauce
1/4	cup	lime juice
1	cup	orange juice
1/2	cup	tequila
2	small	fish Bouillon cubes
1	tablespoon	diet margarine
1	bunch	cilantro
6	cups	water

Directions

- Chop green onions and garlic together, finely. Prepare zest from orange and lime. Squeeze juices. Cut stems from cilantro leaves and discard

- Put the diet margarine in a large nonstick Dutch oven, over medium heat. Add chopped onion and garlic and cook, over medium heat, until just translucent

- Stir in hot pepper sauce, Tequila, zest of lime and orange, and cilantro leaves. Cook, stirring, 2 to3 minutes until the alcohol is evaporating

- Add shrimp, stir once, then remove from heat

- Dissolve bouillon in one cup water. Add to the soup along with all remaining ingredients

- Bring to a simmer and cook several minutes, until the shrimp are just turning pink, serve immediately

- Makes 8 to 9 cups of soup1 1 1/2 cups per serving 170 calories per serving

| CALORIES AS FAT | SODIUM | CHOLESTEROL | FAT Saturated Total | CARBOHYDRATES Refined Complex Sugars Carbohydrates | PROTEIN | DIETARY FIBER | FRUITS & VEGETABLES |

Mexican Shrimp Soup With Crispy Tortilla Strips

6 servings

Ingredients list

2		fish bouillon cubes
5	cups	water
3	large	tomatoes, cut in 8 wedges each
1/2	pound	shrimp (medium, shelled and deveined, tails left on)
6		corn tortillas
2	cups	white wine
1/2	bunch	green onions, cut crossways
1/2	bunch	cilantro, coarsely chopped
1/2	teaspoon	oregano
1		lime (1/2 juice only, other 1/2 cut in 4 wedges)
1	medium	onion
2		cloves garlic
1	teaspoon	red pepper flakes
1	tablespoon	olive oil

Directions

- Mince garlic. Cut onion in very thin wedges and separate layers. Slice green onions. Coarsely chop cilantro

- Cut tortillas into 1/4 inch strips. Heat oven to 350 degrees. Toast tortilla strips on cookie sheet about 10 minutes, until crisp. Set aside.

- In Dutch oven heat olive oil, add onion and garlic and stir over medium heat until onion softens

- Add water, salt, spices, bouillon cubes and bring to a full boil

- Stir in wine, sliced green onions, tomatoes and cilantro, and bring to rolling boil

- Turn down heat, add shrimp and lime juice, and simmer 2 to 3 minutes until shrimp just pink and firm. Serve immediately

- Ladle into heated bowls decorate tops with a handful of tortilla strips and a small lime wedge and serve. Makes 9cups of soup, 1 1/2 cups per serving. 300 calories per serving

100%
50%
0%
CALORIES
AS FAT

SODIUM

CHOLESTEROL

FAT
Saturated Total

CARBOHYDRATES
Refined Complex
Sugars Carbohydrates

PROTEIN

DIETARY FIBER

FRUITS &
VEGETABLES

New Orleans Shrimp Soup
6 servings

Ingredients list

1	pound	medium shrimp in their shells
1/4	cup	Galliano (or other anise flavored liqueur)
1/4	cup	dry sherry
10		cloves garlic
1	bunch	green onions
8	ounces	spinach leaves, 1 package
2	teaspoons	thyme
3	teaspoons	Cajun spice
4	tablespoons	Worcestershire sauce
24	ounces	evaporated skim milk, 2 cans
4	tablespoons	flour
2	tablespoons	diet margarine
1	ounce	Swiss cheese, coarsely grated

Directions

- Cook shrimp in 4 cups water until just simmering. Remove from heat, using slotted spoon to remove shrimp to plate to cool. Reserve cooking broth

- Shell shrimp and devein where necessary. Return shells to the broth while preparing the rest of the soup Reserve peeled shrimp in refrigerator

- Chop green onions medium fine, smash then mince garlic

- Wash and drain spinach and remove stems. Slice leaves crossways at 1 1/2 inch intervals

- Put margarine in a Dutch oven over medium heat. Stir in green onions and garlic and cook, stirring, for 2 to 3 minutes, stir in the flour, and cook, stirring, 2 to 3 more minutes

- Remove from heat. Stir in the sherry, Worcestershire sauce and the spices

- Strain the shrimp broth through a strainer or colander lined with 1 to 2 paper towels. Press down on shells with a wooden spoon to extract all liquid, then discard shells. Stir strained shrimp broth into mixture in Dutch oven

- Return to medium heat. Stir in milk, liqueur, spinach, and prepared shrimp and cook, stirring constantly, until the soup just comes to a simmer

- Serve immediately, sprinkled with grated Swiss cheese

- Makes about 9 to 10 cups of soup, 1 1/2 cups per serving. 265 calories per serving

100%
50%
0%

CALORIES
AS FAT

SODIUM

CHOLESTEROL

FAT
Saturated Total

CARBOHYDRATES
Refined Complex
Sugars Carbohydrates

PROTEIN

DIETARY FIBER

FRUITS &
VEGETABLES

(New Orleans Shrimp Soup)

Orange Orange Roughy Chowder

6 servings

Ingredients list

2		fish bouillon cubes
2		cloves garlic
7	cups	water
1	bunch	green onions
2	large	leeks, white part only
1/4	cup	coarsely chopped fresh cilantro
1/3	cup	frozen orange juice concentrate
1		orange
1	pound	orange roughy fillets (can substitute catfish)
2	tablespoons	olive oil
6		plum tomatoes, seeded and very coarsely chopped
1	ounce	toasted chopped pecans (about 1/4 cup)
2	teaspoons	thyme
2	teaspoons	white pepper
2	tablespoons	flour

Directions

- Slice fish crosswise into 1/2 inch strips. Put the flour in a small closeable plastic bag. Add fish and shake gently until all flour is absorbed. Set aside in the refrigerator.

- Prepare vegetables: chop garlic, slice green onions crosswise, thinly slice leeks crosswise, white part only

- Put olive oil in Dutch oven over medium heat. Add leek, garlic and green onions and cook, stirring, until leek begins to soften 2 to 3 minutes

- Stir in tomatoes and cook, stirring 2 to 3 minutes

- Remove from heat. Add water, bring to a boil and stir in bouillon cubes and frozen orange juice. Simmer 2 to 3 minutes

- Stir in cilantro. Add fish to soup and cook, stirring gently, until the fish starts to turn opaque and white. Ladle into heated bowls and decorate with 1/4 inch thick orange slices, cut in quarters, and sprinkle with toasted pecans. Makes about 9 cups of soup-- 1 1/2 cups per serving. 175 calories per serving

CALORIES AS FAT   SODIUM   CHOLESTEROL   FAT Saturated Total   CARBOHYDRATES Refined Complex Sugars Carbohydrates   PROTEIN   DIETARY FIBER   FRUITS & VEGETABLES

Oysters Rockefeller Soup

Serves six

Ingredients

2	cups	nonfat low sodium chicken broth
2	cans	(12 ounces each) evaporated skim milk
2	cups	2% low-fat milk
1	pint	oysters, canned or fresh, with liquid
1/2	bunch	green onions
2	cloves	garlic
2	tablespoons	grated Romano or Parmesan cheese
2	tablespoons	cornstarch
1	teaspoon	anise seed
1	cup	chopped spinach leaves
1/4	cup	anisette, or similar liqueur
1/3	teaspoon	cayenne pepper
1	teaspoon	freshly ground pepper
1	tablespoon	diet margarine

Directions

- Mince garlic. Wash spinach leaves, pat dry and chop. Chop green onions fine. In Dutch oven melt the 1 tablespoon diet margarine

- Stir in garlic, onion, anise seed, cayenne and black pepper and cook, stirring occasionally, over low heat about 5 minutes until vegetables are soft

- Add spinach, continue to cook 1 to 2 minutes more

- Add oyster liquid and chicken broth to this mixture and stir the evaporated and skim milks into the simmering liquid

- Dilute cornstarch in 1/3 cup water and add slowly to the simmering liquid.

- Cook over low heat, stirring continuously with a wire whisk, until the mixture starts to thicken

- Add oysters and cook 4 to 5 minutes stirring gently with wooden spoon to prevent sticking, oysters should be just firm

- stir in liqueur, remove from heat

- Ladle into warmed cups, sprinkle each with 1/2 tbs. Romano or parmesan cheese and serve

- Makes 8 to 9 cups, about 1 1/3 cups per serving. 260 calories per serving

CALORIES AS FAT

SODIUM

CHOLESTEROL

FAT
Saturated Total

CARBOHYDRATES
Refined Complex
Sugars Carbohydrates

PROTEIN

DIETARY FIBER

FRUITS &
VEGETABLES

Pad Thai Soup

6 servings

Ingredients list

3/4	pound	pork tenderloin, trimmed
1	teaspoon	cornstarch
3	tablespoons	soy sauce lite
1	cup	cabbage, finely shredded
3		carrots
1/2	cup	cilantro leaves
1	cup	fresh bean sprouts (optional)
1	cup	green onions
1/4	teaspoon	red pepper flakes
2		eggs
2	teaspoons	sugar
4	ounces	thin oriental rice noodles
1/2	cup	chunky peanut butter
2	cans	(10 ounces each) low sodium chicken broth
4	cups	water
2	tablespoons	vegetable oil

Directions

- Slice pork tenderloin into thin shreds. Place in a sealable plastic bag. Sprinkle in cornstarch and 2 tablespoons of soy sauce. Mix thoroughly, then place in refrigerator

- Peel and coarsely grate carrots. Wash and very coarsely chop cilantro. Shred cabbage. Pick over and clean bean sprouts. Julienne the green onions. Refrigerate all

- Break noodles into 2 inch segments. Cook in 2 cups water, boiling 6 to 8 minutes. Drain and discard cooking water

- Heat 1 tablespoon oil in a nonstick Dutch oven

- Whip eggs and cook in oil until a firm omelet. Remove onto paper towels, cool, and slice into 1/2 inch strips

- Heat remaining tablespoon oil in a Dutch oven. Cook and stir pork in oil over medium heat until just browning

- Stir in chicken broth, 4 cups water, sugar, and pepper flakes. Simmer 20 minutes. Stir in peanut butter and remaining 1 tablespoon soy sauce

- In 6 shallow bowls, make separate mounds of noodles, carrots, bean sprouts, green onions, cabbage, and omelet strips. You may want to put the bowls on the table first, for a more dramatic presentation, then ladle on soup at the table

- Gently ladle on hot soup, dividing pork shreds evenly. Sprinkle with cilantro
- Makes 6 to 7 cups of soup, about 1 cup per serving (in addition to vegetables in bowls) 400 calories per serving

CALORIES
AS FAT

SODIUM

CHOLESTEROL

FAT
Saturated Total

CARBOHYDRATES
Refined Complex
Sugars Carbohydrates

PROTEIN

DIETARY FIBER

FRUITS &
VEGETABLES

(Pad Thai Soup)

Pizza Supreme Soup*

6 servings

Ingredients list

26	ounces	Healthy Choice® spaghetti sauce
1	bunch	green onions
1	large	green pepper
1	pound	fresh mushrooms
3	ounces	turkey pepperoni (1/2 package)
1	cup	nonfat mozzarella cheese, coarsely grated
2	tablespoons	fresh Parmesan cheese, grated
2 1/4	ounces	(1 can) sliced black olives
2	teaspoons	basil
2	teaspoons	oregano
4	ounces	linguini (1/4 package)
1	tablespoon	olive oil
7	cups	water

Directions

- Wash, trim, and chop green onions. Rinse and slice mushrooms, seed and chop green pepper
- Cut pepperoni slices into quarters. Heat oil in a large Dutch oven. Stir in green onions and green pepper, and cook, over medium heat, stirring until onions are just translucent
- Stir in mushrooms and continue to cook for 3 to 4 more minutes
- Stir in basil, oregano, and black olives, and pepperoni and continue to cook, stirring 3 to 4 more minutes
- Stir in water and spaghetti sauce. Simmer, covered, for 20 minutes
- Break linguini into 1 1/2 to 2 inch pieces. Add to pot and continue to simmer, covered for another 12 to 15 minutes until noodles are cooked
- Ladle into bowls and sprinkle each serving with 1/6 cup Mozzarella and 1 teaspoon Parmesan cheese
- Makes 12 to 13 cups, 2 cups per serving. 250 calories per serving

CALORIES AS FAT   SODIUM   CHOLESTEROL   FAT Saturated Total   CARBOHYDRATES Refined Complex Sugars Carbohydrates   PROTEIN   DIETARY FIBER   FRUITS & VEGETABLES

Plum Chicken Soup*

6 servings

Ingredients list

4		boneless, skinless, chicken breasts
3	stalks	celery
3	medium	carrots
1 1/2	pounds	firm and ripe red plums
1/3	cup	dark brown sugar
1/2	cup	balsamic vinegar
1	teaspoon	thyme
1	tablespoon	oregano
1	teaspoon	pepper
2	tablespoons	soy sauce lite
1	tablespoon	cornstarch
2	cans	low sodium chicken broth
5	cups	water
2	tablespoons	diet margarine

Directions

- Cut chicken breasts crossways into 1/3 inch thick slices. Mix soy sauce and cornstarch with chicken pieces in a sealable plastic bag. Marinate in the refrigerator, 20 minutes or more, while preparing rest of soup

- Peel carrots, wash and cut crosswise into thin rounds, about 1/8 inch. Chop celery medium fine

- Wash plums and cut into eighths, removing seeds

- In a large Dutch oven, melt 1 tablespoon diet margarine over medium heat. Stir in celery and cook until softening. Add carrots and cook 2 to 3 more minutes. Add water, chicken broth, thyme, oregano and pepper. Simmer, covered, while preparing plums and chicken

- In a nonstick frying pan, melt the other tablespoon diet margarine stirfry chicken pieces, all at once, until turning white and firm, 3 to 4 minutes

- Stir in plums and cook another 3 to 4 minutes, until just softening

- Stir in brown sugar and balsamic vinegar, and cook, over medium heat, 1 to 2 minutes more, stirring frequently

- Scrape chicken-plum mixture into simmering soup with a rubber spatula. Continue simmering, covered, about 20 minutes more, stirring occasionally, until flavors are well blended and plums are softened

- Makes about 10 cups of soup, 1 2/3 cups per serving. 235 calories per serving

| CALORIES AS FAT | SODIUM | CHOLESTEROL | FAT
Saturated Total | CARBOHYDRATES
Refined Complex
Sugars Carbohydrates | PROTEIN | DIETARY FIBER | FRUITS &
VEGETABLES |

(Plum Chicken Soup)

Portuguese Steamed Mussel Soup

6 servings

Ingredients list

60		mussels, in shells
1		red bell pepper
1		green bell pepper
1/2	bunch	green onions
1	cup	cilantro, fresh leaves
2	cups	white wine
4		cloves garlic
1/2	cup	lemon juice
8	ounces	clam juice (1 bottle)
2	cups	water
1/2	teaspoon	fresh ground pepper
3		French bread slice, crusty, cut in half
1	tablespoon	olive oil

Directions

- Seed and chop peppers medium fine. Chop onions, reserving green sections. Mince garlic

- Heat oil in a large nonstick frying pan. Add garlic and cook, stirring, 2 to 3 minutes. Add chopped white parts of green onions, and cook, stirring 2 to 3 minutes. Add chopped peppers and cook, stirring 4 to 5 minutes. Remove from heat, and stir in lemon juice. Set aside

- In a 5 to 6 quart steaming pan, mix wine, water and clam juice. Add mussels and cover. Cook over medium high heat until the mussels pop open, about 7 to 10 minutes. Discard any mussels that have not opened

- Divide mussels and the piping hot liquid among 6 heated large bowls. Spoon lemon-pepper sauce over mussels, tuck a bread slice into the side of each bowl and sprinkle liberally with reserved green onions and cilantro

- Makes 6 cups of broth, about 1 cup plus mussels per serving. 300 calories per serving

CALORIES AS FAT • SODIUM • CHOLESTEROL • FAT Saturated Total • CARBOHYDRATES Refined Complex Sugars Carbohydrates • PROTEIN • DIETARY FIBER • FRUITS & VEGETABLES

Raspberry Chicken Soup

6 servings

Ingredients list

3		skinless boneless chicken breasts
1	bunch	green onions
2	tablespoons	flour
2	teaspoons	thyme
2	tablespoons	diet margarine
1/2	cup	raspberry vinegar
2	cans	(two 12 1/2 oz cans) evaporated skim milk
3	cups	water
1/2	teaspoon	salt
1	package	fresh raspberries

Directions

- Cut chicken breasts crossways into 1/4 inch thick ribbons

- Mix flour and thyme in a sealable plastic bag. Add chicken, mixing so surfaces are coated. Put aside in refrigerator

- Chop onion fine

- Melt 1 tablespoon diet margarine in a Dutch oven over medium heat. Cook onion, stirring until translucent

- Add 2nd tablespoon diet margarine. When melted, add floured chicken ribbons and cook, stirring, until just browning

- Stir in vinegar, and cook, stirring, 2 to 3 minutes

- Stir in water, evaporated milk, and salt. Bring to a simmer, and cook simmering for 15 minutes

- Coarsely chop 2/3 of the raspberries and stir them in, simmering for 3 to4 more minutes

- Pour into bowls and garnish with remaining raspberries

- Makes 7 to 8 cups of soup, about 1 1/4 cup per serving, 230 calories per serving

CALORIES AS FAT   SODIUM   CHOLESTEROL   FAT Saturated Total   CARBOHYDRATES Refined Complex Sugars Carbohydrates   PROTEIN   DIETARY FIBER   FRUITS & VEGETABLES

Renee's Herbed Vegetable Cheese Soup*

6 servings

Ingredients list

10 1/2	ounces	Campbell's Healthy Request® cream of chicken soup
10 1/2	ounces	cheddar cheese soup, 1 can
12	ounces	evaporated skim milk, 1 can
16	ounces	frozen mixed vegetables, 1 package
3	medium	red potatoes
3	stalks	chopped celery, w/leaves
2	teaspoons	thyme
2	teaspoons	basil
1	teaspoon	rosemary
1 1/2	teaspoons	ground pepper
3	tablespoons	flour
4	cups	water

Directions

- Put 4 cups of water in nonstick Dutch oven over medium heat
- Wash and coarsely dice potatoes (1/2 inch by 1 inch pieces) leaving peels intact. Simmer in water, covered, about 15 minutes
- Stir in herbs, pepper, chopped celery and frozen vegetables and cook, simmering about 10 more minutes
- Mix flour with about 1/2 cup evaporated milk. Stir in simmering soup. Stir in milk, chicken and cheese soups. Cover and simmer 4 to 5 more minutes, stirring occasionally to prevent sticking, until flavors are blended and vegetables are soft. Do not boil
- Makes 9 to 10 cups of soup, about 1 1/2 cups per serving. 240 calories per serving

CALORIES AS FAT SODIUM CHOLESTEROL FAT Saturated Total CARBOHYDRATES Refined Complex Sugars Carbohydrates PROTEIN DIETARY FIBER FRUITS & VEGETABLES

Roasted Carrot and Ginger Soup

6 servings

Ingredients list

2	pounds	carrots
2	medium	yellow onions
4	cloves	garlic
2	tablespoons	fresh ginger
1/4	cup	fresh ginger, thinly julienned
1 1/2	teaspoons	Chinese 5 spice powder
6	cups	water
2	teaspoons	vegetable bouillon crystals
1/4	cup	corn oil
1		lemon
1/3	cup	nonfat sour cream

Directions

- Peel and julienne the fresh ginger. Grate the remaining ginger. Fry the julienned ginger in 1/4 cup of corn oil until golden brown. Drain on paper. and reserve the used oil for the next step

- Preheat oven to 425 degrees

- Trim and peel carrots. Cut in quarters lengthwise. Place on aluminum foil on a baking sheet. Brush with leftover oil (reserving 2 tablespoons oil) and roast for about 20 minutes, until soft and some browning on the surface

- Chop onions and garlic. Put 2 tablespoons of the reserved oil in a Dutch oven. Cook onions and garlic with grated ginger, in oil, over medium heat, stirring until onions just turning translucent

- Squeeze lemon. Add lemon juice and all other ingredients (*except* sour cream and fried julienne ginger) to a Dutch oven. Bring to a boil. Stir rapidly to break up roasted carrots

- Ladle into 6 bowls, then top each with a tablespoon of nonfat sour cream and a generous sprinkle of fried julienne ginger

- Makes about 8 to 9 cups of soup, 1 1/3 cups per serving. 90 calories per serving

| CALORIES AS FAT | SODIUM | CHOLESTEROL | FAT Saturated Total | CARBOHYDRATES Refined Complex Sugars Carbohydrates | PROTEIN | DIETARY FIBER | FRUITS & VEGETABLES |

Roasted Pepper Soup With Goat Cheese

Serves 6

Ingredients list

2	cans	(10 1/2 ounces each) reduced sodium chicken broth
2	cans	whole green chili peppers (4 ounce cans)
2		yellow bell peppers
1/2	bunch	cilantro
1	tablespoon	olive oil
4	large	cloves garlic
1/3	cup	goat cheese, (or feta cheese) crumbled
4	medium	green or yellow tomatoes
5	cups	water

Directions

- Cut canned green chili into 1/2 inch wide slices

- Seed yellow peppers then cut into 1/2 by 1 1/2 inch strips

- Cut tomatoes into thin wedges and discard any loose seeds

- Chop garlic

- Put oil in Dutch oven and heat to medium high

- Add yellow bell pepper strips and cook, stirring, until just getting limp and browning around the edges. Stir in garlic

- Add green chilies and cook, stirring, 2 more minutes

- Stir in green or yellow tomato wedges and cook, stirring, about 1 minute

- Stir in cilantro leaves, chicken broth and water. Cook, gently stirring occasionally, until soup just comes to a boil. Ladle into bowls. Garnish with 1 tablespoon crumbled goat cheese per serving

- Makes about 7 to 8 cups total, about 1 1/4 cups per serving. 165 calories per serving

| CALORIES AS FAT | SODIUM | CHOLESTEROL | FAT Saturated Total | CARBOHYDRATES Refined Complex Sugars Carbohydrates | PROTEIN | DIETARY FIBER | FRUITS & VEGETABLES |

Roasted Red Pepper Soup

6 servings

Ingredients list

1/2	teaspoon	salt
1		bay leaf
2	medium	yellow onions
2	large	yams
2	medium	carrots
2		cloves garlic
2	teaspoons	fennel seeds
2	teaspoons	dried oregano
2	teaspoons	ground cumin
4		red bell peppers
2		limes
1 1/2	cups	white wine
5	cups	water
1/2	cup	nonfat sour cream
2	cups	cilantro (2 bunches)
1/8	cup	walnuts, toasted
1	tablespoon	grated Parmesan cheese
2	tablespoons	olive oil

Directions

- Peel and chop into chunks: onion, yams, carrots.
- In a large kettle, add water to wine, salt, spices, onion, yam, and carrots, bring to a boil, then reduce to a simmer and cook, covered, for 45 minutes. Cool slightly
- Add the juice from the two limes and puree in batches in the food processor until smooth. Keep warm
- Meanwhile, seed the red bell peppers and roast close to broiler until charred and skin blistering, 5 to 10 minutes per side. Transfer to bowl, cover tightly with plastic wrap and let sit 10 minutes, at which time the skin should slip off easily. Then chop coarsely, reserve.
- Stir chopped roasted peppers into pureed soup mixture and keep warm

- In a separate container of the food processor, puree the washed and dried cilantro leaves, walnuts, Parmesan cheese, coarsely chopped garlic, and olive oil until it becomes a grainy textured pesto

- Pour hot soup into heated bowls. Swirl 1 generous tablespoon nonfat sour cream, and 1/6th of the pesto together in the top center of each bowl to garnish

- Makes about 9 cups. 1 1/2 cup per serving. 240 calories per serving

CALORIES
AS FAT

SODIUM

CHOLESTEROL

FAT
Saturated Total

CARBOHYDRATES
Refined Complex
Sugars Carbohydrates

PROTEIN

DIETARY FIBER

FRUITS &
VEGETABLES

(Roasted Red Pepper Soup)

Salmon Teriyaki Soup

6 servings

Ingredients list

1 1/2	pounds	salmon fillets
1	can	(15 1/2 ounces) carrots
1	can	canned onions
4	ounces	fresh radish sprouts or other tiny sprout
1	tablespoon	ginger, finely grated
1/2	cup	teriyaki sauce, reduced sodium
2	tablespoons	sugar
1	bottle	(8 ounces) clam juice
5	cups	water
1	teaspoon	cornstarch
1	tablespoon	oil

Directions

- Grate ginger. Divide salmon in 6 even portions

- In a plastic sealable bag, mix thoroughly, ginger,1/4 cup reduced sodium teriyaki sauce, 1 tablespoon sugar, and cornstarch. Gently add salmon. Marinate in refrigerator for 1 to 2 hours

- Wash sprouts, drain on paper towels, divide into 6 portions, wrap loosely and refrigerate to crisp

- In a large nonstick Dutch oven. Add oil, sugar, and remaining teriyaki sauce and drained onions (reserve liquid), and cook, stirring, until onions are nicely glazed and browned, trying not to break them up. Add drained carrots (reserve liquid) and cook, stirring gently until glazing, 3 to 4 more minutes. Remove from heat and keep warm

- Add water, the carrots and onions liquid, clam juice, 1/4 cup teriyaki sauce, and drained teriyaki marinade from salmon to the Dutch oven. Bring to a simmer for 6 minutes

- carefully add salmon fillets, to avoid breaking, and simmer covered, another 5 minutes, until salmon is just firm and losing its translucence

- Remove from heat and gently ladle a salmon piece into the center of each of 6 heated bowls

- Surround with carrots and onions, being careful not to break onions. Bring broth to a boil, then divide broth over vegetables and fish, approximately 9 cups, 1 1/2 cups per serving, 250 calories per serving.

- Mound the portions of sprouts over the center of each bowl as a garnish

CALORIES AS FAT   SODIUM   CHOLESTEROL   FAT Saturated Total   CARBOHYDRATES Refined Complex Sugars Carbohydrates   PROTEIN   DIETARY FIBER   FRUITS & VEGETABLES

Santa Fe Corn Chowder

6 servings

Ingredients list

1/2	bunch	green onions
2	stalks	celery
2	cups	whole kernel corn, canned or fresh from 6 medium ears corn
8	ounces	(2 small cans) green chili peppers, chopped
1/2	teaspoon	fresh ground pepper
1	teaspoon	nutmeg
24	ounces	evaporated skim milk (2 cans)
4	small	red potatoes
1	can	(10 1/2 ounces) chicken broth, low sodium
1	tablespoon	oil
2	cups	water
1	tablespoon	sugar
1	tablespoon	flour

Directions

- Slice potatoes crossways into 1/4 inch slices then into quarters, peel left on
- Chop green onions and celery
- Cook the onions and celery in the oil, in a nonstick Dutch oven, stirring, until just translucent, about 4 minutes
- Add potatoes, the can of chicken broth, and the water, and cook, covered, over medium low heat about 15 minutes
- Stir in all other ingredients, except corn, sugar and flour and simmer over low heat 15 minutes, stirring occasionally
- If using fresh corn, hold ears upright and slice off kernels using a sharp knife. Add corn, sugar and flour to soup and simmer for 7 to 8 more minutes, stirring occasionally
- Makes about 9 cups of soup, 1 1/2 cups per serving. 225 calories per serving

CALORIES AS FAT   SODIUM   CHOLESTEROL   FAT Saturated Total   CARBOHYDRATES Refined Complex Sugars Carbohydrates   PROTEIN   DIETARY FIBER   FRUITS & VEGETABLES

Sausage and Lima Soup*

6 servings

Ingredients list

1	pound	turkey Italian sausage
6	medium	plum tomatoes
2	large	yellow onions
4		cloves garlic
3	medium	carrots
3	stalks	celery
1	teaspoon	pepper
2	teaspoons	thyme
1	teaspoon	salt
20	ounces	frozen baby lima beans (2 packages)
8	cups	water
1	tablespoon	diet margarine
1		lemon, juice only

Directions

- Peel and finely chop onions, coarsely chop tomatoes, removing obvious seeds. Peel and chop carrots. Wash and chop celery. Mince garlic

- Melt 1 tablespoon diet margarine in a Dutch oven. Stir in onions and garlic and cook until onions become translucent. Stir in celery and carrots and cook, stirring, 4 to 5 minutes. Stir in tomatoes and cook 1 to 2 minutes

- Add water, salt, pepper, and thyme and lima beans. Simmer, covered, for 20 minutes

- Crumble sausage coarsely. Cook in a nonstick frying pan until nicely browned

- Scrape sausage pan contents into simmering soup, and continue to simmer 15 more minutes, stir in lemon juice

- Makes 9 cups soup, 1 1/2 cups per serving. 365 calories per serving

| CALORIES AS FAT | SODIUM | CHOLESTEROL | FAT Saturated Total | CARBOHYDRATES Refined Complex Sugars Carbohydrates | PROTEIN | DIETARY FIBER | FRUITS & VEGETABLES |

Scallop Fettucine Alfredo Soup

6 servings

Ingredients list

1	pound	scallops
1	pound	sliced mushrooms
8	ounces	fettucine
1	cup	green onions 1 bunch
2	stalks	celery
4		cloves garlic
1	can	(12 ounce can) evaporated skim milk
1	can	(10 1/2 ounces) cheese soup
4	cups	water
1/4	cup	nonfat sour cream
1	tablespoon	diet margarine
2	tablespoons	flour
1	teaspoon	white pepper
1/4	cup	fresh grated Parmesan cheese

Directions

- Chop onions, celery and garlic fine. Rinse and slice mushrooms. Thaw scallops, cut each in half and pat dry

- Put diet margarine in a large Dutch oven over medium heat. Add the chopped onions, celery, and garlic and cook, stirring, until the white parts of the onions becomes just translucent--mixture will be dry. Stir in mushrooms and cook 3 to 4 minutes

- Stir in scallops and cook, stirring, 3 to 4 minutes, until just translucent. Stir flour and pepper into the pan mixture, and cook, stirring, 1 to 2 minutes Add evaporated milk, cheese soup and 4 cups water. Bring to a simmer and set aside

- In a separate saucepan, heat 3 to 4 cups water. Break fettucine into 2 inch lengths and cook 9 to 11 minutes, until just al dente. Drain immediately, and keep warm

- Stir cooked fettucine and sour cream into the soup. Bring to a simmer over medium low heat and simmer 3 to 4 minutes, stirring constantly. Ladle into bowls. Makes 9 cups of soup, 1 1/2 cups per serving. 320 calories per serving

| CALORIES AS FAT | SODIUM | CHOLESTEROL | FAT Saturated Total | CARBOHYDRATES Refined Complex Sugars Carbohydrates | PROTEIN | DIETARY FIBER | FRUITS & VEGETABLES |

Southwest Turkey Stew*

6 servings

Ingredients list

2	cups	leftover turkey, cubed
1	cup	cilantro leaves, loosely packed
1		lime
2	medium	yellow onions
2	medium	green peppers
2	cans	(4 ounces each) green chili peppers, mild or hot
1/2	teaspoon	salt
1	teaspoon	dry mustard
2	teaspoons	cumin seed (or ground cumin)
1	tablespoon	brown sugar
1	can	(11 ounces) whole kernel corn, reduced sodium, with liquid
1	can	pinto beans, with liquid
2	cans	(10 1/2 ounces each) reduced sodium chicken broth
4	cups	water
4	tablespoons	flour
1	tablespoon	olive oil

Directions

- Seed and coarsely chop green pepper. Peel and finely chop onions.

- Put oil in a large Dutch oven. Cook onions over medium heat, stirring, 3 to 4 minutes. Add green peppers and cook, stirring, 3 to 4 more minutes

- Add cumin, salt, sugar, mustard, and green chilies with their liquid. Stir in turkey, and cook, stirring, 1 to 2 more minutes until covered in pan juices. Remove from heat

- Add water, chicken broth, beans and their liquid, chopped cilantro and corn with its liquid. Simmer, covered, for 20 minutes

- Stir flour into a small amount of water until smooth and slowly stir into soup. Simmer an additional 5 minutes until thickening slightly

- Cut lime crossways into 1/8 inch slices making 6, and float a lime slice on top of each bowl to serve

- Makes 12 cups, 2 cups per serving. 490 calories per serving

CALORIES AS FAT — SODIUM — CHOLESTEROL — FAT Saturated Total — CARBOHYDRATES Refined Complex Sugars Carbohydrates — PROTEIN — DIETARY FIBER — FRUITS & VEGETABLES

Spicy Chinese Beef Soup

6 servings

Ingredients list

2	pounds	beef chuck, well trimmed
4	tablespoons	soy sauce lite
6	medium	carrots
1	bunch	green onions
1/2	cup	dry sherry
1	tablespoon	sugar
1	tablespoon	five spice powder
4	cloves	garlic
4	slices	fresh ginger root
1/4	teaspoon	crushed red pepper
8	cups	water
1/2	cup	white rice, raw
1	tablespoon	oil

Directions

- Finely chop onions, carrots and garlic

- Cut beef into 1inch cubes, removing all fat. Brown in oil in a medium Dutch oven. Remove to plate, leaving drippings in pan

- Stir onions, garlic, carrots and red pepper into pan drippings and cook, stirring, 4 to 5 minutes. Add meat back in

- Stir in all other ingredients, except rice

- Simmer, covered, over low heat for 1 hour, or until the meat is very tender. (Meanwhile prepare rice, without salt, according to package directions)

- Mound one small scoop of rice into the bottom of each bowl

- Ladle soup with sliced meat over it. Makes about 9 cups of soup, 1 1/2 cups per serving. 450 calories per serving

The Doctor Cooks
Soups

Surprise Vichyssoises

6 servings

Ingredients list

3		leeks, white parts only
1	bunch	green onions
1	tablespoon	oil
4	medium	baking potatoes
2		ripe pears
1	tablespoon	lemon juice
1	bunch	watercress
12	ounces	(1 can) evaporated skimmed milk
1/2	cup	nonfat sour cream
6	cups	water
1/2	teaspoon	salt

Directions

- Wash leeks. Rinse thoroughly under running water to remove all sand. Slices white parts of leeks crosswise into 1/2 inch slices, pat dry. Chop green onions, reserving 1/3 cup of chopped green part for garnish

- Heat oil in Dutch oven. Cook onions and leeks over medium heat, stirring until just turning translucent. About 5 minutes

- Peel potatoes and cut into chunks. Add water and potatoes. Simmer, covered, until they fall apart when tested with a fork. Cool mixture until manageable

- Peel and chop ripe pears and cover thoroughly with lemon juice to avoid turning brown. Add to cooked potato mixture

- Chop watercress leaves. Add 1/2 to potato mixture, reserving the other half for garnish

- Blend or food process the potato mixture (in portions if necessary) until smooth. Return to pan. Add the evaporated skim milk and cook, over very low heat 5 to 7 minutes until flavors are blended. Do not allow to boil. Cool and start to chill

- Stir in sour cream and reserved chopped water cress

- Serve chilled, garnished with reserved chopped green onions

- Makes about 9 cups of soup, 1 1/2 cups per serving. 205 calories per serving

| CALORIES AS FAT | SODIUM | CHOLESTEROL | FAT Saturated Total | CARBOHYDRATES Refined Complex Sugars Carbohydrates | PROTEIN | DIETARY FIBER | FRUITS & VEGETABLES |

Sweet and Spicy Spaghetti Squash Soup

6 servings

Ingredients list

1	tablespoon	olive oil
1	medium	onion
2		cloves garlic
1	stalk	celery with leaves
2	pounds	spaghetti squash
4	ounces	frozen orange juice concentrate (half can)
2		Italian tomatoes
21	ounces	chicken broth low sodium (two 10 1/2 cans)
1	teaspoon	red pepper flakes
1/2	teaspoon	cinnamon
3	cups	water
1	ounce	sliced almonds, packaged

Directions

- Chop onion, celery. Mince garlic. Chop tomatoes coarsely, removing seeds.

- Lightly toast almonds on baking sheet in 350 degree oven (watch carefully to avoid burning) set aside

- Put olive oil in Dutch oven over medium heat. Stir in onion, celery, and garlic, and cook stirring until onion softens (about 5 minutes)

- Add water and chicken broth and remove from heat. Cut washed spaghetti squash in half longways--cook, covered with microwave proof wrap, in microwave 6 to 7 minutes on high (until squash strings easily when raked with a fork) Scrape all squash out of shell

- Add juice, pepper flakes, cinnamon, tomatoes and red peppers to broth mixture. Bring to a boil

- Stir in squash and simmer 15 minutes, covered.

- Remove 1 cup of vegetables to food processor. Blend until smooth, then add back to soup

- Ladle soup into heated soup bowls, garnish by sprinkling with toasted almonds

- Makes 8 to 9 cups of soup, about 1 1/2 cups per serving. 125 calories per serving.

CALORIES AS FAT   SODIUM   CHOLESTEROL   FAT
Saturated Total   CARBOHYDRATES
Refined Complex
Sugars Carbohydrates   PROTEIN   DIETARY FIBER   FRUITS &
VEGETABLES

Taco Soup*

6 servings

Ingredients list

1/2	pound	ground beef, extra lean
1	cup	cilantro, loosely packed
1	bunch	green onions
2		cloves garlic
29	ounces	Mexican style stewed tomatoes, 2 cans
1	medium	green pepper
3	medium	carrots
1	package	taco seasoning mix, low sodium
5	cups	water
1/2	cup	nonfat sour cream
3		corn tortillas
2	tablespoons	vegetable oil

Directions

- Seed and chop green pepper and grate carrots

- Heat 1 tablespoon oil in a large Dutch oven

- Chop onions and garlic together, add to Dutch oven with ground beef, chopped green pepper, and grated carrot

- Stir together over medium heat until meat is just browning. Add taco seasoning and stir 3 more minutes. Add cilantro, canned tomatoes, salsa, water, and chili powder. Cover and simmer for 30 minutes

- Meanwhile, brush corn tortillas with oil, cut into halves, then quarters, then 1/8ths--place on a cookie sheet in a preheated 450 degree oven, and brown, turning once, 3 to 4 minutes per side--watch carefully to avoid burning

- Ladle soup into bowls. Top each serving with a generous tablespoon of nonfat sour cream and 4 tortilla wedges

- Makes about 11 cups 1 3/4 cups per serving. 350 calories per serving

CALORIES AS FAT   SODIUM   CHOLESTEROL   FAT Saturated Total   CARBOHYDRATES Refined Complex Sugars Carbohydrates   PROTEIN   DIETARY FIBER   FRUITS & VEGETABLES

The Doctor Cooks

Soups

Tetrazini Turkey Soup*

6 servings

Ingredients list

2	cups	cubed leftover turkey
4	ounces	linguine
1	pound	sliced mushrooms
8	ounces	pimiento (two 4 ounce jars)
2	medium	yellow onions
4	ounces	green chili peppers, 1 can, mild
3	stalks	celery
10	ounces	cream of chicken, Healthy Request (1 can)
12	ounces	evaporated skim milk (1 can)
1	tablespoon	diet margarine
1	teaspoon	white pepper
3	teaspoons	marjoram
5	cups	water
1/3	cup	lowfat cheddar cheese

Directions

- Peel and chop onions medium fine. Chop celery medium fine. Rinse and slice mushrooms

- Put diet margarine in a large nonstick Dutch oven over medium heat. Add celery and onion and cook, stirring constantly, until the onions become translucent, 3 to 4 minutes

- Add mushrooms and continue to cook, stirring 3 to 4 minutes. Remove from heat

- Stir in spices, chili peppers and their liquid, pimientos and their liquid and all other ingredients except the shredded cheddar cheese and linguine

- In a separate pot, start 4 cups of water boiling, break linguini into 2 inch pieces and cook, 10 to 11 minutes, until just tender, drain and add to soup pot

- Stir soup pot while bringing to a slow simmer. Simmer, covered 10 to 15 minutes, stirring every minute or so. Do not boil

- Ladle into bowls and garnish with shredded cheddar cheese

- Makes 9 cups of soup, 1 1/2 cups per serving. 330 calories per serving

CALORIES AS FAT   SODIUM   CHOLESTEROL   FAT Saturated Total   CARBOHYDRATES Refined Complex Sugars Carbohydrates   PROTEIN   DIETARY FIBER   FRUITS & VEGETABLES

Texas Hash Soup*

6 servings

Ingredients list

1/2	pound	ground round
32	ounces	tomato juice (1 bottle)
14 1/2	ounces	canned, diced tomatoes, no salt added
1	bunch	green onions
1	medium	yellow onion
2	large	green peppers
1	tablespoon	chili powder
1/2	teaspoon	cinnamon
1	teaspoon	sugar
1	teaspoon	salt
2	tablespoons	Worcestershire sauce
1/2	cup	uncooked rice
5	cups	water

Directions

- Trim and chop green onions. Seed and dice green peppers
- Brown round steak in a nonstick Dutch oven in its own juices, stirring occasionally
- Add chopped green onions and diced green peppers. Cook, stirring frequently, over medium low heat, until peppers are softening and the onions become translucent, 4 to 5 minutes
- Stir in all other ingredients, simmer, covered, for about 30 minutes, until the rice becomes soft and has split open
- Makes about 12 cups of soup, 2 cups per serving. 210 calories per serving

CALORIES AS FAT   SODIUM   CHOLESTEROL   FAT Saturated Total   CARBOHYDRATES Refined Complex Sugars Carbohydrates   PROTEIN   DIETARY FIBER   FRUITS & VEGETABLES

Three Bean Chili Mac Soup*

6 servings

Ingredients list

1	tablespoon	olive oil
2	medium	yellow onions
6	cloves	garlic
4	ounces	chili peppers, canned
1	tablespoon	chili powder
1	tablespoon	cumin
2	cans	(14 1/2 ounces each) Mexican stewed tomatoes
1	can	red kidney beans, drained and rinsed
1	can	black beans, drained and rinsed
1	can	pinto beans, drained and rinsed
1	cup	pasta, shells or macaroni
1/2	cup	Colby Reduced Fat, grated
6	cups	water

Directions

- Chop garlic. Put oil in a large Dutch oven. Cook garlic, stirring, over medium heat, until just starting to brown. Remove from heat
- Stir in all other ingredients except pasta and grated cheese. Bring to a boil. Reduce heat and simmer 15 to 20 minutes, covered
- Stir in pasta, and simmer, covered, for another 15 minutes
- Ladle into hot bowls, sprinkled liberally with grated cheese
- Makes about 12 cups of soup, 2 cups per serving. 500 calories per serving

CALORIES AS FAT   SODIUM   CHOLESTEROL   FAT Saturated Total   CARBOHYDRATES Refined Complex Sugars Carbohydrates   PROTEIN   DIETARY FIBER   FRUITS & VEGETABLES

Tofu Crab Soup

6 servings

Ingredients list

1	can	(8 ounces) crab meat, canned
2	teaspoons	corn oil
1	bunch	green onions
1	tablespoon	ginger root, shredded
1	tablespoon	dry sherry
2	cans	(10 1/2 ounces each) chicken broth low sodium nonfat
2	cups	water
1	cup	tofu diced
3	tablespoons	cornstarch, mix w/ water
1	tablespoon	vinegar
1	teaspoon	salt
2	cups	fresh spinach, sliced in 1 inch wide strips
1		egg substitute (equivalent to two eggs)

Directions

- Grate ginger. Slice green onions thinly crossways.

- Put oil in a nonstick Dutch oven over medium heat. Add ginger and green onions, stir, cooking about 1 minute

- Stir in spinach and cook until slightly wilted. Stir in dry sherry

- Add the cans of chicken broth and two cups water. Bring to a boil

- Stir in the cornstarch mixture, vinegar, and crabmeat with its juices. Cook until thickened and clear, several minutes

- Reduce heat and stir in diced bean curd (tofu) pieces. Add up to 1 teaspoon salt (or less to taste). Cook until just returns to boil

- Stir in egg beater in a swirling motion, 1 to 2 times around the pan. Remove from heat and keep warm

- Makes 6 to 7 cups, 1 cups per serving, 110 calories per serving

Tomato Sweet Corn Chowder

6 servings

Ingredients list

2	tablespoons	diet margarine
1	bunch	green onions
2		cloves garlic
6		ears of corn
3	cups	skim milk
12	ounces	evaporated skim milk (1 can)
1	teaspoon	salt
1	teaspoon	fresh ground pepper
3		ripe tomatoes
1	cup	water

Directions

- Dice tomatoes removing obvious seeds
- Slice the corn off the cobs, collect juice and kernels. Chop whites and green parts of onions separately, mince garlic
- Melt diet margarine in Dutch oven, add garlic and whites of onions and cook, stirring until soft, 2 to 3 minutes
- Stir in milks, salt, pepper, tomato, and fresh corn with its juices, and water
- Heat to just below boiling
- Cook, stirring occasionally 7 to 8 minutes
- Ladle into bowls and sprinkle liberally with green onion tops
- Makes about 6 cups of soup, 1 cup per serving. 170 calories per serving

CALORIES AS FAT   SODIUM   CHOLESTEROL   FAT Saturated Total   CARBOHYDRATES Refined Complex Sugars Carbohydrates   PROTEIN   DIETARY FIBER   FRUITS & VEGETABLES

Tom Yung Kung Thai Shrimp Soup

Serves six

Ingredients list

4	cups	chicken broth low sodium
1 1/2	cup	water
1/2	tablespoon	cooking oil
2		cloves garlic
1	pound	shrimp * see note
1/2		green onions
16	leaves	fresh cilantro
1	cup	straw mushrooms **see note
1		lime juice only
2		Italian tomatoes, diced, seeds remove
2	teaspoons	soy sauce, low sodium
1	teaspoon	molasses
2	teaspoons	catsup
3	tablespoons	Thai fish sauce
1		chili pepper (or 1/2 teaspoon dried red pepper flakes)

*medium, raw, peeled, veined, with tails left on
**1 can drained straw mushrooms, or 1 cup thinly sliced fresh mushrooms

Directions

- Mince garlic, wash, trim and slice green onions thinly crosswise, wash and pick off leaves of cilantro, drain straw mushrooms (or thinly sliced fresh mushrooms)

- Cook garlic in oil in Dutch oven. Add mushrooms and cook, stirring, 2 to 3 minutes

- Add chicken broth, and water, then stir in all other ingredients except green onions, shrimp, cilantro, and lime juice

- Bring to a boil. Reduce heat and simmer 5 minutes

- Stir in, shrimp, green onions, cilantro, and lime juice. Simmer only until shrimp are just turning pink. Don't overcook. Serve immediately

- Makes 7 to 8 cups of soup, about 1 1/4 cups per serving. 135 calories per serving

CALORIES AS FAT   SODIUM   CHOLESTEROL   FAT Saturated Total   CARBOHYDRATES Refined Complex Sugars Carbohydrates   PROTEIN   DIETARY FIBER   FRUITS & VEGETABLES

Tortilla Soup

Serves six

Ingredients

2		skinless boneless chicken breasts
1 1/2	quarts	cold water
1	large	roasted and unpeeled onion
8		roasted and unpeeled garlic cloves
1		bay leaf
1/2	teaspoon	marjoram
1/2	teaspoon	thyme
1/2	teaspoon	oregano
1	small	jalapeno * see note
2	tablespoons	fresh lime juice
6		corn tortillas, cut in strips
1/4	cup	vegetable oil
4		green onions, sliced crosswise
3	medium	tomatoes, cut into eighths
2		limes, cut in wedges

*or use 1 teaspoon red pepper flakes for less heat

Directions

- Combine first 8 ingredients in large saucepan, bring to a boil
- Reduce heat so liquid barely simmers and cook until juices run clear when chicken is pierced with fork (about 40 minutes)
- Remove the chicken from pan and cool
- Boil broth until reduced by 1/4
- Strain through paper towel lined colander
- Skim fat from broth and discard fat
- Cut chicken into bite-size pieces, return meat to broth
- Slice small hot pepper crosswise into thin slices
- Heat 1/4 cup oil in large heavy skillet over medium heat
- Fry tortilla strips in batches (do not crowd) until golden (about 30 seconds) drain on paper towels

- Cook in same skillet, white parts of crosscut green onions (reserve green parts for garnishing) until just beginning to soften (about 5 minutes) stirring frequently
- Add tomato, sliced jalapeno pepper, and lime juice cook stirring for 2 minutes
- Mix into soup, heat to gentle boil
- Season with salt and pepper
- Ladle soup into bowls
- Add handful of fried tortilla strips to the top of each bowl, and sprinkle with reserved green parts of green onions
- Serve immediately, passing lime wedges separately
- Makes 9 to 10 cups soup, 1 1/2 cups per serving, 250 calories per serving

CALORIES AS FAT   SODIUM   CHOLESTEROL   FAT
Saturated Total   CARBOHYDRATES
Refined Complex
Sugars Carbohydrates   PROTEIN   DIETARY FIBER   FRUITS &
VEGETABLES

(Tortilla Soup)

Tuna Noodle Casserole Soup*

6 servings

Ingredients list

12	ounces	tuna (light salt) in water (2 cans)
14 1/2	ounces	green beans, canned w/liquid
4	ounce jar	pimientos
10 1/2	ounces	cream of chicken, Campbell's® Healthy Request
10 1/2	ounces	cream of mushroom, Campbell's® Healthy Request
12	ounces	evaporated skim milk (1 can)
3	cups	water
1/2	pound	fresh mushrooms, sliced
1/2	bunch	green onions
2	stalks	celery
1	teaspoon	thyme
1	tablespoon	diet margarine
1	cup	uncooked egg noodles
6	tablespoons	French fried onions, canned

Directions

- Wash celery, green onions and mushrooms. Chop celery and onions medium fine, slice mushrooms if not already sliced

- Put 1 tablespoon diet margarine in a large nonstick Dutch oven. Cook vegetables over medium heat, stirring frequently 3 to 5 minutes

- Add pimientos, thyme, soups, green beans with their liquid, tuna with its liquid, water and evaporated milk. Cook over low heat, stirring occasionally, 10 to 15 minutes

- Meanwhile, boil noodles in about 1 quart water, no salt, until just soft, drain

- Stir noodles into soup, and simmer 3 to 4 minutes, stirring frequently

- Ladle into bowls and sprinkle 1 tablespoon canned French fried onions on top of each serving

- Makes 12 cups of soup, 2 cups of soup per serving. 250 calories per serving

CALORIES AS FAT SODIUM CHOLESTEROL FAT Saturated Total CARBOHYDRATES Refined Complex Sugars Carbohydrates PROTEIN DIETARY FIBER FRUITS & VEGETABLES